Roscommon County Library

D1339591

Roscommon County Library Service

WITHDRAWN

FROM STOCK

BATISTA UNLEASHED

World
Wrestling
Entertainment®
BOOKS

BATISTA
UNLEASHED

Dave Batista

with Jeremy Roberts

POCKET BOOKS

New York   London   Toronto   Sydney

ROSCOMMON

Pocket Books
An imprint of Simon & Schuster, Ltd.
Africa House, 64–78 Kingsway,
London WC2B 6AH

Copyright © 2007 by World Wrestling Entertainment, Inc.
All Rights Reserved.

World Wrestling Entertainment, the names of all World Wrestling
Entertainment televised and live programming, talent names, images,
likenesses, slogans and wrestling moves, and all World Wrestling
Entertainment logos and trademarks are the exclusive property of World
Wrestling Entertainment, Inc. Nothing in this book may be reproduced
in any manner without the express written consent of World Wrestling
Entertainment, Inc.

This book is a publication of Pocket Books, a division of Simon & Schuster,
Ltd., under exclusive license from World Wrestling Entertainment, Inc.

All rights reserved, including the right to reproduce this book or portions
thereof in any form whatsoever. For information address Pocket Books
Africa House,
64–78 Kingsway,
London WC2B 6AH

Photos on pages 3–4, 36–7, 64–5, 104–5, 168–9, 188–9, 240–1, 302–3
Courtesy of Jeremy Roberts. Photos on pages 9, 15, 43, 44, 51, 53, 55, 72, 87,
89, 91, 177, 184, 212, 232, 271 Courtesy of the Bautista family.

All other photos and images Copyright © 2007 World Wrestling
Entertainment, Inc. All Rights Reserved.

First Pocket Books UK hardcover edition November 2007

POCKET and colophon are registered trademarks of
Simon & Schuster, Ltd.

Designed by Richard Oriolo

Visit us on the World Wide Web
http://www.simonsays.co.uk
http://www.wwe.com

Printed and bound in Great Britain

10 9 8 7 6 5 4 3 2 1

ISBN: 978-1-84739-065-3

A CIP catalogue record for this book
is available from the British Library

I'd like to dedicate this book to the
people who made it happen for me:
Rich, Jonathan, Paul, and my beloved Angelia.
I couldn't have done it without any of you.
Thank you, and I love you.

CONTENTS

On the Road: Leaving St. Louis 3

o n e DEAD MEN 5

On the Road: Carbondale 37

t w o WEIGHTS 41

On the Road: Somewhere in Illinois 65

t h r e e DUES 69

On the Road: Urbana 105

f o u r EVOLUTION 111

On the Road: Flashback—*WrestleMania 21*   153

five **CHAMPION**   155

On the Road: Chicago, Bound for Omaha   169

six **THE LOVE OF MY LIFE**   175

On the Road: Halfway to Sioux City   189

seven *SMACKDOWN!*   195

On the Road: Sioux City   221

eight **COLLATERAL DAMAGE**   223

On the Road: Omaha   241

nine **BACK ON TOP**   245

On the Road: Omaha   265

ten **ROAD STORIES**   267

On the Road: Omaha   303

BATISTA UNLEASHED

M4

On the Road 2/3/07

LEAVING ST. LOUIS

It's Saturday afternoon, February 3, 2007.

I've just arrived at Lambert International Airport in St. Louis, Missouri. It's a little after one, and I have a show tonight at seven thirty. That sounds like a hell of a lot of time, but the show is in Carbondale, Illinois, a hundred-something miles away. Not only do I have to get myself over there, but I want to find a gym and a tanning salon beforehand. And I have to eat, because I'm starved.

There's a problem with the car rental—the car hasn't been reserved. It takes quite a while to work it out. Finally, the computer coughs out the right paperwork and I'm on the road.

So much of this business is on the road, traveling. As the highway unwinds, I have a million things on my mind, including this book, which the publisher has been after me to finish for a few months now.

When they first asked me to write it, I was flattered, but I really wasn't sure about doing it.

What do people want to know about me? And why do

they want to know? I don't pretend to be a deep thinker. I don't talk that much. When I do, I say what I honestly feel, and I say it plainly, in just a few words. That's rare today, maybe—enough to have gotten me in trouble at different times—but that's not a reason to write a book.

I went ahead and agreed to it, but even then I hesitated, stopped and started. Finally, I figured I would just plunge in and see what came of it. Doing it has made me think about things that have happened to me—events that rushed past me at the time. And it made me think about pro wrestling, why people connect to it, and how wrestlers go about creating our art every night.

I'm still not sure that's enough reason to write a book. But this is it.

One

DEAD MEN

Every story has a beginning. Mine is in Washington, D.C., in 1969.
Washington, D.C., in the sixties, seventies, and eighties
was one of the poorest places in the country. Murder was common. Crack cocaine was just getting its start. Life expectancy for
kids was worse than in many third world countries. The politi-
cians were corrupt, homelessness was at its peak, and even law-
abiding people viewed the police as the enemy.

But to me, it was home.

I won't say I was unaffected by the poverty and crime around me when I grew up. It's not like I lived on a safe cul-de-sac around the corner from the ghetto, either: three people died at different times in my front yard before I was nine. But to me, D.C. wasn't the life-sucking hellhole it was for a lot of people. And the big reason for that was my mom.

FAMILY

I was born January 18, 1969.

For some strange reason, the date is a big controversy in the wrestling world. At some point very early in my career, someone wrote a story somewhere saying that I had been born in 1966. That year seems to have stuck with a lot of people for some reason. There have been other dates published, too. There have been so many, in fact, that when I give the right date, some people think I'm lying about my age.

I swear to God, it's like it's a big deal.

Just last week some guy told my girlfriend I was lying about my age, that I wasn't really thirty-eight, that I was forty-two. Maybe he was trying to pick her up, I don't know.

I don't lie about my birth date—I try not to lie about anything, but especially not that. It's no secret that I came to the business really late. I was almost thirty when I got into wrestling. That's real old for a wrestler starting out. I never lied about my age then, so it would be really crazy to lie now. And if I *was* going to lie about my age, I wouldn't say I was thirty-eight. I'd knock at least five more years off.

I have a sister, who was born about a year later than I was. Our parents weren't very original when it came to naming us. I was named after my father, David Michael Bautista. I'm Dave Junior. My sister was named after my mother, Donna Raye Bautista. She's a junior, too. It made it easier for people to remember our names.

(I spell my name Batista for wrestling, but on my birth certificate it has a *u* after the first *a*.)

My father was born in Washington, D.C., but his family was from the

Philippines, and as a wrestler I've always felt a strong bond with the fans in the Philippines because of that family connection. His father, my granddad, was in the army; he didn't talk much about what he did, but I know he was in World War II and was wounded or hurt in some way. The family legends have him down as a hell-raiser when he was young, but I don't know much more than that.

I always heard that he was a real ladies' man, and that he got into some trouble in San Francisco when he was younger. Supposedly he was running numbers for gangsters and did something for which, for some reason or another, they wanted to kill him. Whatever it was that he did, trouble chased him out of town and he came east.

Those bad days were long gone by the time I came along, and he never told me about them, even though I was his favorite and he wasn't afraid to show it. On the contrary: he used to brag about it.

According to the family stories, my grandfather would never really hold any of my cousins or me when we were babies. He wasn't the nurturing type. But then one day my mom had to run to grab something burning or something like that and she just threw me in my grandfather's arms. His face lit up. By the time she came back to get me, he and I had bonded somehow. From that day, I was his favorite grandchild. I still remember him asking how much I loved him and holding my hands out to say, "This much!"

When he died in 1988, it just broke my heart. He's buried in Arlington Cemetery, an honor reserved for men and women who have served our country.

My grandfather had a bunch of jobs in the Washington, D.C., area, but I only knew him as a barber. He had his own shop in Oxen Hill, Maryland, an old-fashioned place with four chairs in it. He had to be one of the most popular guys in the neighborhood. Everybody knew him. You'd go into a McDonald's with him or just walk down the block and everyone would say hello. He was very friendly and very well liked.

He was also a very generous grandfather. When I was around six or seven, we lived real close to the shop, maybe a few blocks away. I'd go into the shop and sit in his chair, just hanging out. He'd give me lollipops all day. My cousin Anthony, who was a little older than me, would stop by, too. Sometimes, my grandfather would give us a few bucks and we'd go to Toys "R" Us. It was right across the street.

It was funny. For a while we had a regular little scam going, me and my cousin. We'd buy the toys and play with them; then, after we got a little tired of them, we'd break them and take them back.

"This toy's broken," we'd tell them.

So they'd take them back on exchange and we'd get more toys.

Anthony and I were close while we were growing up, very close. He was my only male relative in my generation, and for a while I lived with him, his sister, and their parents. So that made him the closest thing I had to a brother as a kid. He could be a bully sometimes, like any older brother. Nothing too serious: he would tease me until I cried, things like that. But I still loved him. I always looked up to him and wanted to be like him.

Unfortunately, he died a few years ago in a terrible car accident. It really shook up the family. I still miss him.

LESBIAN AND DEMOCRAT

My mom's father, Kenneth Mullins, was in the service, too. He was in the Marines during the Korean War and got both the Purple Heart and Silver Star. Both of my grandfathers were men to look up to and feel proud of, because of their service to our country.

I was never very close to the Greek side of my family, mostly because my mother wasn't. But she still tells the story of how when I was born, all of her Greek relatives came over to visit. They started yelling when they saw me: "He's Greek! He's Greek!"

They were all happy and proud, pointing out this and that facial feature that they said was due to Greek genes.

Of course, the Filipino side of the family was there, and they got pretty upset. They claimed I looked more Filipino than Greek.

My mother calls herself the black sheep of her family. She was always a lot more liberal than her parents: Granddad was a conservative, she was a left-wing Democrat. After she and my father separated, she fell in love with a woman. At some point, her father caught her in bed with another woman, which was how he first found out that she was a lesbian. I think

Me and my
granddad
Kenneth.

she may regret that a little bit, but she and her dad have gotten closer over
the years, and I know there's a lot of love between them now. She still
jokes, though, that she did two things that disappointed her father: told
him that she was a Democrat, and told him that she was a lesbian.

"Of the two, being a Democrat was far, far worse," she says. "Not even
close as far as he was concerned."

My mother's sexual orientation was never an issue for me. She made it clear that she loved my sister and me, and there was never any doubt in my mind about that.

THE GONG SHOW

My father was a different story.

He and my mom had been high school sweethearts and got married right out of school. They were both really young. I don't know exactly what happened, but it seems clear to me that my father wasn't ready to be a father. They did try, on and off, to get together and get back together. Some of those attempts were halfhearted. But I don't really remember them sharing affection, hugging or kissing or anything like that.

I remember us all watching *The Gong Show* together. That was about the extent of family togetherness for my mom and dad.

In all the years after my parents split up, basically since I was able to walk, I never felt that my father supported us.

My mother says now, "You can't get blood from a stone."

I don't know about that. It seemed to me he was making a pretty good living at the time, and we just lived in a dump. We had nothing. I always felt something was wrong with that.

We recently talked for the first time in, let me see, over ten years. But it was really awkward. I felt as if I'd been forced into talking to him. Things are still hard between us. I don't really think he ever wanted to be a father. He told me recently that he never knew how to be a father. That was fuckin' obvious. But he could have taken a better shot at it.

He said it made him sad that we hadn't talked in a long while and didn't have any contact. I told him that it didn't make me sad. I didn't miss him. The reason I didn't miss him was that I never really felt like I had a father. I knew he was there, I knew he was my father, but I grew up without the feeling of having a father around. My mother played the role of mother and father, and she was what I knew and what I was used to. He was just never there. I really didn't miss him in my life because he was never there.

Knowing what kind of father he was makes me know what kind of father I don't want to be. My own first marriage didn't last that long—only long enough to have two kids—and honestly, we only got married because my wife was pregnant. But I never felt like I didn't want to be a dad. I always wanted to be there for my children. I loved them. And still do. It's a hard thing to put into words. It's something you really just have to feel. And I feel it very strongly.

WASHINGTON, D.C.

D.C. was—still is—pretty rough.

I don't know how much you know about D.C., but basically it's subdivided into four quadrants—northeast, southeast, southwest, northwest. There are a lot of nice neighborhoods in D.C., and some of the city is being gentrified, but at the time we lived there it was a pretty violent ghetto. We lived in southeast, not that far from the Capitol. The area had a pretty high homicide rate: guns, knives, even fists were used to kill people regularly. The number of violent deaths climbed each year until 1991, when they peaked at 482 across the city. That's one murder for every 1,250 people—a couple of deaths on each block, each year.

I asked my mother about what it was like back then, and she said that she wouldn't let us out of the house Friday nights. She used to call them "hooker weekends." Even during the week we were not supposed to go out of the yard.

But as a kid, I don't remember ever feeling unsafe. It was ethnically diverse, which was great. There were a lot of different backgrounds there. Black, white, Hispanic—a little bit of everything. My mom says that we may have been the only white people in some of the places we lived, and I'm pretty sure she was right. The funny thing is, I really wasn't that aware of it. Really wasn't.

I always had such fun living in D.C. I knew then and know now that there was a lot of bad stuff: I remember people getting shot, and a crowd of people beating up one guy right in front of our house. But I had real good friends. And when you're a kid, that's really what's most important.

We had this neighborhood game, nobody's ever heard of it probably outside of D.C., but we called it "hot bread and butter." It was like tag. What we'd do, we'd get a belt, a big belt, and we'd hide it. We'd have a base, just like you have in hide-and-seek. All the kids would look for the belt, and whoever found it would yell "hot bread and butter." Then he or she got to chase around the other kids and beat them with the belt until they got to the base.

We played regular games, too. A lot of touch football on the street. We'd stay out all night in the summertime, just playing and having fun. There were tons of kids, and I don't remember there ever being gang problems or stuff like that. The gang problems started a few years later, fortunately, after I'd grown up.

The first fight I ever got into was in D.C. Some kid stole my skateboard. Well, a bunch of my friends caught him with it; one of them ran up to my house, got me, and said, "Come get your skateboard." I went down there. The kid tried to take my skateboard back and I punched him in the head.

He didn't bother me again, but I'm sure he stole somebody else's skateboard the next day.

My mother tells this story about how one time she was taking a shower—she must have been getting ready to go to work—and all of a sudden she heard gunshots. Well, she grabbed a towel and ran to the window to see where we were. We weren't in the yard, so she started to scream, "DJ! DJ! Baby Donna! Baby Donna!"

She and the rest of my family call me DJ, which stands for Dave Junior, and at the time she called my sister Baby Donna, which I guess sounded better than Donna Junior.

Anyway, just as she was probably about to have a heart attack, my sister came flying around the corner, followed by me. There were these two guys right behind us. One was a big fat guy who was the neighborhood drug dealer. When I say he was fat, I mean he was *really* fat—obese, actually. And he was being chased by this skinny guy who had a gun and was shooting.

Somehow we got into the house without being hit. My mom can tell the story now and have you rolling on the floor laughing, but it sure wasn't funny to her then.

My mom worked at this place called District Photo that was several towns away in Maryland. They developed film. She worked nights, and without anyone else to take care of us, she had to leave us in the house by ourselves. At one place, the upstairs neighbor, the guy who owned the house, was around if we needed him. But usually we were just there by ourselves, my sister and I. We'd put ourselves to bed.

My mother would take a bus to get there and back. Usually. If the bus didn't come on the way back—and a lot of times it would just stop running without explanation—she had to hitchhike home around three in the morning. There were a few times when somebody stopped and she just sensed something was wrong, so she didn't get in the car—which meant she had to walk home. That was a hell of a lot better than taking a chance, though.

The thing I remember from her working there were the big company picnics. Those were kind of cool. That's where I actually had my first drink of beer, when I was eight or nine. I have a picture of it, too: I have a big cup of beer in my hand and am wearing a KISS belt buckle. Real 1970s.

KISS was a hot rock band at the time. Gene Simmons, Paul Stanley, Ace Frehley, and Peter Criss were the band members. They wore face paint, played heavy metal, and were huge at the time. They also had reputations as wild men offstage, Frehley especially.

I don't remember the beer, but I do remember not really caring for it much. I still don't. I'll drink Jack Daniel's over beer any day of the week.

HAPPY WEEKENDS

My mother was always trying to brighten things up for us. I remember her waking us up one morning and packing us into the car—this was one of the few times when we had a car—and taking us to get donuts and watch the sun come up at the Jefferson Memorial. That was always her favorite memorial in the city.

She had this philosophy that weekends should be different from the rest of the workweek, and she tried to make them special for us even though she didn't have a lot of money to work with. She invented what she called "happy weekends." We'd go on a little trip or she would make us these little sundae snacks in special cups she bought someplace. Cool stuff like that is what I remember when I think about being young and living in D.C.

We didn't have a typical household where you come home and eat dinner together; none of that. In fact, there were a lot of times when we didn't eat at all. My mom would stock up during sales, buy things like beans and cereal. That's what we'd eat. One day my mom was broke but had bought these beans with I guess some vegetables. She was making us a big pot of navy bean soup that was supposed to last us all week. It was all we had to eat.

But she burnt the soup. Burnt the *shit* out of it. But because that was all we had, that was what we ate. The whole week. Burnt bean soup.

Everybody around us was struggling to make do. We weren't the only hungry kids around by any means.

One time my sister was at a friend's house across the street. They had a father and a mother, but they also had five kids, and they didn't have anything to eat that night. So the mother called over to our house and said, "I talked to your daughter and I know you're having tough times, too. I'll be honest, we don't have much to give our kids to eat tonight. But I can make two sheets of biscuits, if you have something to go with it."

"I have butter and jelly and apple butter," my mom told her.

We went over and we pigged out. It was like a picnic. The adults told us we were having dessert for dinner, Kool-Aid and biscuits and jelly. We thought it was fun.

Sometime around then, President Reagan said on television that no one went hungry in America. That kind of set my mother off. She started yelling at the TV, "Why don't you walk out your fuckin' door? Why don't you walk down here?"

The White House was literally just up the street. It wouldn't have been hard for anyone in D.C. to realize that, hell yes, people were hungry in America. All you had to do was take a walk. Whether you were the president or anyone else, it wouldn't have been hard to see hunger anywhere in D.C.

WITHOUT TEARS FOR THE DEAD

I had a lot of fun growing up in D.C., and as I said, to me it didn't seem any more dangerous than anywhere else. We couldn't afford toys, we didn't have video games or computers—so we spent all our time outside. We'd make up games and run around all night in the summertime, until one or two in the morning. It was all the neighborhood kids. I never felt unsafe doing it. I knew I was different, because I was white and my friends were black, but I never felt different. I fit in. And it always seemed like there were ten or twenty kids around, whether it was playing football in

Me and my sister, Donna.

the street or just hanging out. God, we'd walk for miles to go to a public swimming pool.

Again, I'd be the only white kid there. But it was one of those things where no one ever really bothered me. And if they did, it was no big deal. Nobody was getting shot or stabbed or anything; you were just handling things with your fists.

But my mom remembers the city a lot differently than I do. She came from there, and I know she loved it. Probably still does. But her perspective at the time was as a mom with kids, and she wanted to protect them. She didn't think much of anything in the city was fun.

A couple of things convinced her she wouldn't be able to stay in D.C. One time a guy was trying to shoot someone on the block nearby and, instead of hitting the person he had the beef with, he hit an innocent girl. People in the neighborhood grabbed him and were taking him to the highway overpass nearby to throw him off. My mother called the police and managed to convince them to get there just in time to stop the mob from killing the guy.

This was around 1976. My mother went out to San Francisco to get settled, find a job and a place to live. My sister and I stayed with my father's parents. That sucked ass. My grandmother was mean, nasty, and abusive. I remember her slapping me across the face more than anything else; that's my memory of her. One time, she got pissed at me because I said something nasty to my sister, so she took a big key ring full of keys and threw it at me and hit me in the face with it. Oh yeah, she was a real bitch.

Luckily, I only stayed with her for just a few months. First my sister and then I went out to join my mother. The new place was nice, especially compared to where we had lived, but we weren't there very long—less than a year—before my father came out for a visit.

He and my mom tried to patch things up. Not only that, but he actually convinced her that we should all move back east and live with him in Maryland, close to D.C. but not quite in it.

We moved back, but it didn't last long: my mother says three weeks. Anyway, my parents split again and my mom, who not only was broke but without a job, moved us back to D.C.

Things had actually gotten worse in the year or so that we'd been gone. Once, someone was found dead in our front yard, and another was found very close by. But it was the third guy that really set her off. This stranger's death made her decide we had to move out of there. She was worried, really worried, that one of us might end up being next. There was so much going on she couldn't protect us from it all. And she was even more worried about what the place was doing to us.

The murder happened on a Friday night. She came out of the house and found this man with a bullet hole in his head. She ran back in and called the police and an ambulance. Forty-five minutes later, neither the police nor the ambulance was there.

In the meantime, all the kids from the neighborhood had heard that something was going on and came around to see. I was there, and I believe my sister was, too. We were all standing around looking at this poor guy who was dying. I think some of us were even telling jokes. My mother got real upset and pulled us aside.

"The day you can stand over a man who is dying in the street and you don't feel compassion and you don't have a tear in your eye," she told us, "it's time for us to go."

We moved back to San Francisco right after that.

WELFARE

For a while when I was little, my mother didn't have a job and I remember her being on welfare. She *hated* being on welfare. *Hated it.* But she had two kids and had to do something to keep them from starving. She got a job, though it wasn't well paying, and earned extra money cleaning people's houses, anything to keep us going and not take welfare. The jobs started getting a little better—we weren't really that well off, but we had nowhere to go but up. She started working for a courier service, and then eventually DHL. DHL came with union benefits. She called it a "godsend" when she got it. In fact, she still works for them, though while I'm writing this she's on an unpaid family leave of absence. To this day, she's a very proud member of Teamster Local 85 in San Francisco. She's just really very thankful for everything they've done for her.

We lived on Fourteenth Street near Divisadero Street and Castro. School was down the block, and there were two parks—Buena Vista and

The Warlord.

Duboce—close by. Our home, like most of the apartments there, was a big flat. At least it seemed huge to us at the time, maybe because we didn't have any furniture.

My mom found a mattress that my sister and I shared for a while. We had milk crates to sit on in the kitchen, and industrial-size wire spools for a kitchen table. We had that for years. Somebody told me recently that those spools are real chic now. We were cool before our time.

Mom used to go to the thrift store and get clothes for us. I remember one pair of shoes I had worn through on the bottom, and I had to tape cardboard inside of them so my feet didn't get wet.

MY MOM GOT US THROUGH

I think my mom was really strong, as strong as you can imagine. And loving, too; just real loving. But she was stern when she had to be.

You can't get away with this anymore, but I'll tell you, she'd not only beat us if we were bad, she'd whip the shit out of us. She'd put us over her lap and spank the shit out of us. Her children knew right from wrong. And we weren't supposed to talk back. That was one of her big rules.

I remember one time in San Francisco, I was in trouble for something, I don't know what it was. She was just yelling at me. Anyway, I thought she left and I was alone in the apartment. So I started cussing, "I hate that fucking bitch!" And I turned around and there she was.

Oh man, she laid into me. She beat the shit out of me. She knocked me on the ground. It's funny now, but I think I may still have the bruises.

But she was also very loving and affectionate. She was never afraid to tell us that she loved us or to hug us. I think that's a real important thing for parents. They have to show their kids they love them.

WARLORD

I watched a bit of pro wrestling as a kid. I think my favorite wrestler was The Warlord. Sometimes I get teased about that. Most people don't know who The Warlord was. If you ask them who their favorite was when they were a kid, they'll always say Hulk Hogan or Macho Man, Ric Flair, or maybe Dusty Rhodes.

I say The Warlord and people say, "Who?"

Terry Szopinski was The Warlord. He started in World Championship Wrestling in 1986, where he was managed by Baby Doll and then Paul Jones. This was back before Ted Turner bought the wrestling franchise and created the WCW that was so popular as a rival to World Wrestling Federation in the 1990s. Terry wrestled there for a few years, and then went to World Wrestling Federation.

During his career, he teamed with Barbarian as The Powers of Pain, and some of his most memorable matches involved feuds with The Hart Foundation—Bret Hart and Jim Neidhart—and the Road Warriors. In real life, the Road Warriors—Hawk and the original Animal—were friends and had encouraged Terry to get into wrestling. At points during his career he was known for wearing a reverse Mohawk haircut and face paint; his signature moves included the Warlord Lariat—a clothesline he administered from a dive—and the Warlord Lock, which was a variation on the full nelson. Like most wrestlers, he worked as both a babyface and a heel, though it was probably as a heel that he earned his greatest recognition.

I think I admired him because he was the most massive human being I had ever seen. I always looked up to the big guys. I thought they were just incredible.

A THING FOR HEELS

When you're a kid, sometimes the wrestlers who make the biggest impact are the heels. You remember them because they're your mortal enemy. You want to squish 'em like a bug when you grow up.

You know one wrestler I really hated when I was a little kid? Mr. Fuji. I despised Mr. Fuji. I don't know why. I just despised him. And guys like Rick Rude. I always hated Rick Rude. He was a *great* heel. He was so arrogant; he was just perfect.

Speaking of perfect: I hated Mr. Perfect, too. I hated him. Arrogant prick.

Mr. Fuji is probably another wrestler today's generation doesn't know. His real name was Harry Fujiwara, and he began his career as a wrestler, though at some point he became popular as a manager. His peak as a wrestler, a bit before my time, came as a tag team partner in World Wrestling Federation, where his partners included Professor Toru Tanaka and Mr. Saito. He was inducted into the WWE Hall of Fame in 2007.

I think Rick Rude is still pretty well known to older fans, especially if you give them the full name, "Ravishing" Rick Rude. He was a big-time heel, so overconfident and arrogant that you couldn't help but hope he would slip on a banana peel or something on his way to the ring. He was a star in both WCW and World Wrestling Federation in the late eighties and nineties. Tragically, he died in 1999 from heart failure. He was only forty.

Mr. Perfect—well, the name says it all. Curt Hennig, of course, wrestled as Mr. Perfect for a portion of his career when he was with World Wrestling Federation. He was the son of Larry "The Ax" Hennig. He's a Minneapolis boy who wrestled for a long time with the old AWA before joining WWE. He held the Intercontinental title in 1990 and in 1991, losing it in a memorable match to Bret Hart. Unfortunately for those of us who admired his wrestling style even while hating his heel character, injuries cut short his ring career with WWE in the 1990s. He continued not only as a commentator but occasionally appeared with regional franchises. A hall of famer, he passed away in 2003.

When I think about those guys now and remember how much I hated them, I realize just how good they really were.

We didn't get a chance to go to many live wrestling events when I was little. Money was tight, and there were other priorities, like food. My mom still talks about taking us to see a cable telecast of one of the *WrestleMania*s in San Francisco when I was little. I believe I saw the Wild Samoans there, and maybe Hulk Hogan, but I don't remember it all that well.

Which kind of disappoints my mom, since it cost ten dollars to take us—huge money for us at the time.

Roscommon County Library Service

WITHDRAWN FROM STOCK

COUNTY LIBRARY SERVICE
796
81209.2
ROSCOMMON
4349991.

GOING BAD

School in San Francisco was a lot different than D.C. For one thing, we weren't the only white kids in class anymore. The school was only a block away from our house and was really new and more modern. It was a nice place, as far as the building went.

But I never really liked school, in D.C. or in San Francisco. The first time I ever skipped school—we called it ditching—I must have been in first or second grade. The older I got, the more I'd ditch.

Not that it was a good thing to do, or that it made any sense. One time, a couple of friends and I ditched school the day the class was going on a field trip to the zoo. So what did we do? We went to the zoo. We followed them around, watching them. They were there, we were there; it wasn't like we were getting out of schoolwork. So tell me how that made sense. But I guess it seemed like fun at the time.

The schools I was in tried to catch up to me, but usually they didn't do all that good a job. One time, I think it was sixth grade, the principal called the house looking for my mom. I answered the phone and tried to convince him that I was her. I don't think it worked, but I did skip just about that entire year.

Cutting class meant we had a lot of extra free time. I can't say that we spent it all that wisely. We spent a lot of hours riding around, on the bus and the cable cars. When I was a kid, you could ride the bus all day long for a nickel, and get bus transfers to the cable cars. Sometimes if the conductor or bus driver asked for the fare and you didn't have it, you'd just jump off.

After Fourteenth Street, we moved to a much rougher neighborhood, and I began getting into trouble more. It was about then, sixth grade I think, when I realized that a lot of the kids were hanging out with their own cliques, according to either race or ethnic background. Mexican kids were hanging out with Mexican kids, the blacks were with the blacks, the whites were with the whites. I didn't fit in anywhere exactly. I was white, but I'd grown up with black and Hispanic kids and they were my closest friends. I started hanging out with all the blacks and Mexicans. I kind of blended in there best.

We were living across the street from some projects, or what is now called government-subsidized housing. They were more than a little bit rough. This was the first time I started realizing anything about gangs. They weren't doing drive-bys or stuff like that back then, but there was a lot of stealing, a lot of fighting, stuff like that. I started doing it, too. We'd take whatever we could get our hands on. Food, bikes, money, whatever.

I remember once we stole a motorcycle when we were ten or eleven. I snuck out of the house. It must have been about three or four in the morning. We broke into this garage of another house and stole the bike. There were three of us, and because we didn't want to start it up in the garage, we carried it out. Then my friend Carl took off on the bike and left me and the other kid running behind him.

Most of what we did, though, wasn't that bad. We'd hang around, or go onto rooftops and try to look into people's apartments. I remember a couple of times watching people have sex. That was the sort of thing we did to pass the time.

Every once in a while, the other kids would tease me about being Filipino. They'd call me a Flip. So I'd have to come back with, "Fuck you, fucking beaner." We could spend quite a bit of time teasing one another. It seems funny—goofy—now.

Another thing we'd do for fun was go to the Tenderloin district, where all the hookers were. We'd stay out till three or four in the morning, teasing hookers and watching them take johns back to the alley. We'd try to get the women mad at us, then take off. It was just funny, teasing the hookers. None of us were interested in them in a sexual way. They didn't show us the facts of life or anything like that. In fact, I was kind of a late bloomer, especially compared to the kids I knew.

Most of the kids I hung out with were a little older than me. I was a little bigger than kids my age, taller, so it didn't seem strange. We fought with our fists, no weapons, no knives, and nobody ever had a gun. There were some fights, but the worst that ever happened was a black eye here and there.

In those days, especially growing up there, I think everybody got into fights. It was part of being a kid. It wasn't like it is now. You never worried about someone coming back and blowing your head off. You had a fight and that was it. It was over. At worst, you might have two or three fights with the same guy, but that would usually settle things.

JOURNEY TO THE 'BURBS

By the time I was thirteen, I started getting in a lot more trouble for skipping school. I also got arrested for petty stuff. I'd get detention or juvenile hall, but the punishment wasn't severe; I never spent more than a day in jail.

I wasn't stealing or breaking the law to get back at anyone or because I was mad or anything like that. I was stealing because all my friends were doing it. It was no big deal. It just wasn't out of the norm. It was what you did. Good, bad, angry, sad—nothing like that entered into it.

My mother, of course, hated it. She had to be the disciplinarian, and I think she worried that she would become like her own mother, who was abusive. But I also know that she was worried about what might happen to me. She worried I might end up dead.

There was one time when some kids came to the house looking to beat me up for something stupid—I forget what it was—but she stepped in and kicked them out before anything happened. Something like that has to scare you as a parent.

One night, a bunch of friends and I stole some bikes and rode over the Golden Gate Bridge to Sausalito. Cops picked us up and they called my mom to come get me. She flipped. She'd finally had enough. She called up my father and told him I was going to end up dead or in prison. So I went to live with him in Arlington, Virginia.

Which was really fucking weird.

I went from being kind of a street thug to living in suburbia. It was culture shock. Actually Arlington is very nice, but at the time I didn't know how to live there. The town was quiet by nine o'clock. It drove me nuts.

When I moved there, I was in seventh grade and I think I was thirteen at the time. The school was Thomas Jefferson Middle School, and I did so poorly they sent me to a special program at another school. Basically, I did the same thing in school in Arlington that I had done in San Francisco: I ditched class all the time. My grades were terrible. But now I wasn't riding streetcars or hanging out with wannabe gang members. I discovered girls.

My house became the party house, mostly because my dad was never home. He'd give me like twenty bucks for the weekend and just take off. I'd be on my own. I'd have my friends over and it would be one big party.

I had a best friend named Nelson. We hit it off right away; he was kind of an oddball, like me. He had his ear pierced in seventh grade. Now that's pretty common, but back then it was considered daring if you were a boy. So of course I got my ear pierced when I saw his. We thought we were so cool. We were seventh-grade players.

The schools tried to get me in line. I was suspended for skipping, but it didn't have all that much effect. Nothing really did. I continued to hate class, and more times than not I just ditched it.

I remember the first time I got suspended, my dad beat the shit out of me with his weight-lifting belt. He was really pissed at me. My father wasn't as tall as I am today, but he was still a pretty good size, about six foot and two hundred pounds. He was lifting weights and working out, so when he hit me with the weight belt, it had some heft to it.

But I took it. I always felt like I had to stand up to him. The next time I got in trouble, I knew I was in for it. So before he came home, I went and took the belt out and threw it on his bed and waited. Why? Fuck him, that's why.

He didn't really know how to deal with me. But maybe nobody would have. It wasn't that I was stealing cars or doing dope or anything really, really bad. But I was definitely a thug, and everyone was afraid of where I was headed.

LOVE

I did have some positive things happening for me, some good influences in my life. One was my girlfriend, Susan Nah, whom I started dating in seventh grade. She was a year ahead of me, and by the time I got to Washington-Lee High School, my life just about revolved around her.

She was a very good student, in a lot of ways your typical girl next door. I fell in love with her the moment I saw her. You would, too, if you saw her. She was five feet tall and never grew taller than that, so we were a real odd couple. She wasn't your typical knockout, but adorably cute. And really smart.

Her dad worked for the government and her mom was a teacher. They tried to be really positive influences in my life. Later on, I had her mother as my teacher in history class. I can't say whether I ever skipped or not, but I did think she was a very good teacher and I did respect her a lot.

I wasn't a rebel or anything. I just never felt like I fit in at high school. I always felt like an oddball, different. People would be doing one thing and I would want to do another. Like sports and dancing: when everybody I knew wanted to try out for football or play baseball, I wanted to be a break-dancer.

Break dancing was a 1980s street thing where a dancer would show off his or her moves. You'd touch the ground with your head or hands in a real high-energy dance to rap and hip-hop, which were pretty new at the time. I met a bunch of kids doing it and just got into it. We used to go into D.C. and that's what we'd do all night. It was cool back then. Big revues and just a bunch of kids hanging out.

Someone recently pointed out that some of the moves I now make in my entrance with WWE can be traced back to break dancing. I'm not conscious of it. They used to have me come out real simple, no personality, you're-a-killer-just-go-to-the-ring kind of thing. When Vince McMahon had me open up a bit, put more personality into my character, it kind of came in. It was just a part of me.

A lot of the music I remember from back when I was a kid are songs by the Fat Boys and Grandmaster Flash, which is all old-school rap now. As a matter of fact, I still like their music. I've always had very eclectic tastes; I can go from listening to heavy metal to hard rap. And I have a real appreciation for opera, especially Pavarotti. I have some of his stuff on my iPod.

My first year in high school I played football, though only because I felt like that was what I was supposed to do. That's what all the other cool kids were doing. I gave it a try. I was just terrible at it. I played tight end and I was just rotten. I had no idea what I was doing. I played defensive end my junior year and I wasn't that much better.

GROUP HOME

In my freshman year of high school, I started getting into a lot of fights. One was over my girlfriend, because this kid was hitting on her, but mostly I was just hotheaded. I was charged with assault because of one of these fights. One thing led to another, and in the end I was sent to a group home. It was punishment, I guess, but the idea was supposed to be positive; this place was supposed to straighten kids out.

It wasn't that bad, actually. Maybe ten or twelve guys lived there, with counselors. They tried to get you to live a structured life. You didn't have much freedom, and you had to follow the rules. I didn't necessarily like it, but I didn't hate it either.

My counselor when I was there was a young man named Arthur MacNeil. We used to call him Mac. He was a really positive influence on my life. He was one of those guys who really made an impact—I still remember him all these years later. He was a very positive person, very helpful. We bonded and I considered him a lot more than just a counselor. He was a friend. Every so often he will pop into my head and I wonder how he's doing these days. Well, I hope.

By the time I left the group home, I was pretty straightened out. I was on a good path. I didn't stay on it, but I was moving in the right direction. I went back to living with my dad.

Before I went home for good, I was allowed to go to my father's for a weekend. It was my sixteenth birthday, I think, so I threw myself a birthday party. It was one of the best parties of my life. I invited maybe twenty people and two hundred showed up. It was one of those crazy nights. I got into a fistfight with one of my best friends, that's how wasted I was. We had this huge Ping-Pong table and it got trashed. By the end of the weekend the Ping-Pong table was in so many pieces, we just got rid of it. The house was a complete wreck. There were holes in the walls, and mirrors were broken. I spent one whole day with my friends trying to make repairs.

Then I had to go back to the group home.

My father got back to the house sometime after me. When he did, the door was wide open. He had jewelry missing and, of course, the place was still pretty trashed. But what really upset him was the fact that the Ping-Pong table was missing. "Where's the fucking Ping-Pong table?!" he said.

LEARNING TO WRESTLE

About the time I was going into my junior year at high school, we moved and I was switched to Wakefield High School. That's where I discovered amateur wrestling. Richard Salas and some other friends of mine were on the wrestling team and they encouraged me to come out because I was pretty big by this time, about six two, 185 pounds. I did okay. I believe I won our junior varsity tournament that year and even finished fifth in the district championships. That wasn't great, of course, but it wasn't horrible either, especially considering that I'd never wrestled before in my life.

Wrestling is an individual sport, but for me it was a real team thing. I forged great friendships. Some of my friends from back then are still my friends today. When you're working out so many hours with guys and just working your asses off together, you just bond. You encourage each other, and it makes you closer.

That's similar to what we have now in the locker room at *SmackDown!* and WWE. We're all busting our asses on the road every week. We keep each other going.

ASTHMA

One of the things I had to deal with as a wrestler was my asthma.

I've been asthmatic since I was born. I'm not a doctor, obviously, but to give you a little bit of background, asthma attacks your airways by irritating the tubes that carry air in and out of your lungs. When you have an attack, the airways get inflamed and they narrow. That means less oxygen can get into your lungs and you start having trouble breathing. At this point, no one has found a cure for asthma, but there are different ways of controlling it. Asthma attacks vary from person to person. They're generally caused or made worse by allergies. That's the cause in my case. I have a bunch of common allergies to animals, pollen, and cigarette smoke, things like that. Most of us who have asthma have learned how to control it.

While I'd had asthma in D.C., when we first moved to San Francisco it was so bad I spent a lot of time in the emergency room—up to two or three times a week. In fact, we were there so much that someone from social services came and checked up on us, just to make sure something bad wasn't going down. My mother would wash the floors, make sure that we used only foam pillows, all those sorts of things.

Asthma runs in the family. It has hindered me a little bit from time to time, but it never stopped me from wanting to compete, or getting out there and being active. While a lot of times I've been given a bad rap for not being in good cardiovascular shape, the truth is I don't have good wind because I'm asthmatic. It can catch up to me in the ring, but I just have to deal with it as best I can.

To this day, I always have an inhaler close by. I take a drug to help keep it under control. I've had episodes where it's been pretty bad, but I've never had an attack where I was in serious jeopardy. It's something I'm used to. It's just part of my life.

A MOTIVATOR

Back in high school, we had this great wrestling coach: Coach McIntyre. I don't remember his first name—it was always "Coach Mac" as far as I was concerned. He wasn't the kind of guy that would scream or anything, but he could really motivate you. He'd just talk to you, man to man, and you'd want to do your best.

I remember one time, we had a meet and my opponent had forfeited. I went out with my head gear unstrapped and in shorts and a T-shirt. When I got back, he didn't rip me apart about it. He just took me aside.

"When I was a kid, whether I had a forfeit or not, I went out on the mat and I was prepared," he told me. "I was ready to wrestle. You should have a little more respect for the team. I'd appreciate it if you'd do that."

That was really a strong way of teaching. It seems simple, but it really got the point across, and I always made sure I was dressed properly from then on. I respected him. He treated me like someone who deserved respect and should show it in return. It's a powerful thing, respect.

I think more than anything, what I remember about wrestling in high school was how important the work ethic was. How hard you had to work to be good. It's a lesson that I took with me, and that I still believe in.

In my senior year, I was really looking forward to wrestling again. But my grades were so bad that I ended up not being academically eligible. That was a real bad year in general.

KICKED OUT

Things at home got real rough when my father decided to remarry around my freshman year. It was a shock to everybody, even my mother. They had never actually gotten divorced. He called her up one day and asked if she would sign some papers. She went along with it; I don't think she thought she had much choice.

Then just about right away, my father and his new wife were expecting a baby. They decided there wasn't room for me in the house.

My dad wanted me to go out and live with my mom. She didn't want me to come out there. I don't think she could really afford to have me go back out there, and she didn't have the room for me at the time. She might also have been worried that I would slip back into my old problems. So I ended up moving in with a friend of mine and his family in the Arlington area, boarding with them while still going to Wakefield High. I think my dad gave them a hundred bucks a month or something like that.

My father turned my room at his house into a nursery. It sucked bigtime. My dad had never really been there for me, so it wasn't a complete shocker. But you know, here I was going into my last year of high school, and it was more the idea of the thing, just how low it all seemed.

In the meantime, my girlfriend, who was a year older than me, went off to college. I started fucking up again, even worse than before. I ditched school pretty regularly.

STAY IN SCHOOL

The truth is, I never finished my senior year in high school.

It's painful and embarrassing as hell for me to admit it, but I never graduated.

I've regretted it my whole life since. I wish I had taken my education more seriously. I always felt I could have done well if I applied myself. But I just didn't care. Education meant absolutely nothing to me. It's one of the biggest mistakes of my life.

I tell both of my daughters, I make a living with my body because I have to. If I get injured, God forbid, I have nothing to fall back on. I'll end up as a bouncer in a nightclub again. I will always regret not taking my education seriously. I really believe I could have done something better with myself.

These days, kids always ask, "How can I become a professional wrestler?" I tell them to go to school first. Because the odds that you're going to make it are very, very slight. And even if you do, it's a hard-knock life. If you have no education, you're screwed. Which is the case with a lot of athletes. Often, they're pushed through or given degrees they haven't earned, which isn't much better than not getting a diploma at all.

The worst part about it is, I *could* have finished high school. I was in twelfth grade. When I felt like it, I could get good grades. Teachers let me make up assignments when I missed something. I wasn't stupid, except when it came to making good decisions about my life. I was just a fuck-up and decided to do whatever I wanted. I didn't apply myself, and to this day I regret it.

If you're reading this book and you're in high school or you know someone in high school, take my advice: *Stay in school. Learn as much as you possibly can.*

WORK

Instead of going to school, I hung out. And I went to work—after a fashion.

I started out with a real good friend named Ben. He'd been a friend of mine for six years. I haven't seen him in a long time, but he's one of those people who I swear if I ran into we'd talk to each other just as if we had seen each other yesterday. That's how close we were. He was definitely no angel, but he never let me down. He was, is, a great friend.

I would help him out here and there, making sure he was okay and he was getting paid. In a way, I was like a bodyguard. I was big and people tended not to bother him when I was around.

In January 1989, I was arrested for shooting a firearm into an occupied dwelling. Someone unloaded a shotgun at a house belonging to some kids who had robbed Ben, and naturally I was suspected. The cops came over and arrested me. But they didn't have any proof, not even the gun. The people in the house hadn't seen who'd done it. Really, it took balls for them to call the cops in the first place.

I went to jail for about a week before the charges were finally dropped and I was let go.

It didn't take long for me to figure out jail wasn't where I wanted to be. I was always a 49ers buff, and I watched the 49ers–Bengals Super Bowl from jail. It just broke my heart. But it wasn't quite enough to get me straight, not at that point.

DRUG CHARGE

Not too long after that—in fact, I believe I was out on bail—I was with Ben in a car when we were pulled over. There were drugs in the car, and the cops arrested us both. The quantity was just enough to charge us with distribution, which is a pretty serious crime. If they'd gone really hard on me, I could have been looking at a jail sentence of several years.

But I didn't have a criminal record, and my friend vouched for me, saying the drugs weren't mine. They put me in a drug program and gave me a year probation, and said if I did okay they would go back to court and reduce the charge to possession of drug paraphernalia. So that's what I did.

It's funny now, I guess, but when I was arrested on that drug charge, I made bail right away. But as I was being bailed out, the first bail bondsman revoked his bail. He thought I was too high risk, so he took his bond back. I came down, thinking I was going to be released, only to find out I wasn't getting out at all. As you can guess, I was pretty upset. Eventually, I did make bail and was let out.

Today, if you look at my rap sheet, you'll see I was convicted for possessing drug paraphernalia, which is a misdemeanor. I'm not making light of it—those were terrible, stupid things to do, and no one should ever, ever follow my example.

DRUGS AND PARANOIA

People hear about a drug conviction and they automatically think, Oh, that person did a lot of drugs. But in my case, I never really did a lot of drugs. I've just never really been into that.

Smoking weed or marijuana always made me paranoid. I really hate that feeling. One time Ben asked me to hold some stuff for him.

I was home by myself and bored as hell, so I smoked some weed. Then I got paranoid. I was looking out the window every ten minutes, I was so afraid someone was watching me. I moved Ben's stuff about fifty times, going through the house all night. That's what I did, in between eating a gallon of ice cream and a pot of chili.

And while there have certainly been a good number of exceptions, for the most part I'm not even much of a drinker. To this day, I drink here and there when I go out, but not all that much. At home, I rarely drink at all. I've just never enjoyed it all that much.

ASSAULT CASE DROPPED

I was charged with assault one other time, but those charges were also dropped.

It was another instance involving a friend of mine named Chris. We were at a shopping mall, and Chris wanted to get his ear pierced, but he didn't have any money. So we went up to this kid who was the younger brother of this girl we knew, and started picking on him a little. We told him to give Chris some money so he could get his ear pierced. The kid was kind of scared. He said he didn't have any money, but that he had some at home.

Chris didn't want him riding in the car, so we stuffed him in the trunk of his car. It seemed funny at the time, but it was awful. Chris was really hitting this kid a lot. He threw steak knives at his feet, then stole some jewelry from the kid's house.

The police investigated and arrested both of us. I didn't know Chris stole the jewelry at the time—he didn't tell me until later on. He ended up giving all the jewelry back and they dropped the charges.

It seemed funny at the time, but as I'm writing this I realize it sounds horrible: stuffing a kid in the trunk of a car, beating him up, and stealing his mom's jewelry.

Jesus Christ, what was I thinking?

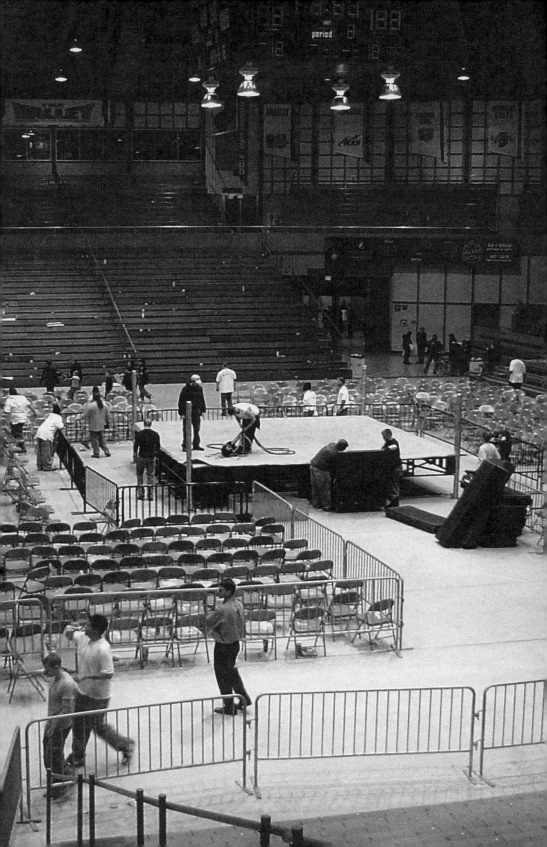

CARBONDALE

By the time I get to Carbondale, touch up my tan, and grab something to eat, it's after five and I'm running late. It's still winter and it's pretty dark; the end of town where the college arena is located seems deserted. I spend a few minutes circling around the campus, looking for the building and then trying to figure out where I'm supposed to go. Finally I see our *SmackDown!* truck parked near the building.

When we do a live television show, we need a whole fleet of trucks to carry everything we use—the ring, set, lights, television cameras, and whatnot. We have a small army of production people who come in and set up, do the show, and strip it back down. But house shows—wrestling events that aren't televised—are different. *SmackDown!* house shows have one semitrailer that carries all the equipment. It's a tight squeeze, but they get it all in.

WWE is one company with three different "brands" of wrestling, each centered around a television show: *Raw, SmackDown!* and ECW. (At the time that I'm writing this, ECW is traveling with *SmackDown!* and we tape our shows together.)

The weekly television shows are actually just a small part of a wrestler's schedule. In a typical week, *SmackDown!* might do three house shows—Saturday, Sunday, and Monday—and then the TV show Tuesday. The last day is always television day; it tends to be longer and more intense than the others. After that, we get a travel day and then maybe two days off. But a lot of us have appearances on those off days and other commitments that soak up the time. And we're on the road just about every week of the year, not just in America but in Europe and Asia as well.

When I finally find the right parking lot, Todd, who's head of security for the show, directs me to a good parking spot near the door. Todd's a good guy; he and his brother Jimmy watch out for us before and after the show, making sure that we're not bothered and that things stay calm. They're really nice guys, though I wouldn't screw with them if I were you.

I really depend on the security guys a lot. One of my closest friends on the road was one of our security coordinators, Jimmy Noonan. He's not with us anymore, unfortunately, but I really enjoyed working and traveling with him. I don't have any great stories about Jimmy, but he was always saying something funny, cracking me up. He's just a typical New York wiseass. He could be grouchy in a funny way. We got close on the road and I really felt like I trusted myself in his hands.

Inside, the crew has already set up the ring. Our producer, John Law, has a small table near one of the stands. He'll work the sound system from there, cuing the intros and the incidental music. Right now he's briefing the locals who will handle the spotlights, telling them what to do and mostly trying to get them to relax. There are two spots tonight, and they're not going to have to do anything real fancy—just follow us out to the ring.

The show is being held at the Southern Illinois University Arena, a basketball gymnasium that fits about ten thousand people and dates to the early sixties. It's plain and a little dated—the school has plans for a new arena. But its small size gets the fans real close; it's one of those places where you can sense the crowd from the moment you step out of the dressing room . . .

Two

WEIGHTS

Things started to turn around for me the year I was put on probation. It didn't happen all at once, and it wasn't really because I was on probation.

The big thing was: I became a father.

LIFTING

I started lifting weights probably when I was seventeen years old. My dad had weights around the house and I just started getting into it. I was a skinny kid, tall but skinny. I remember being teased because I was so vascular, really veiny. You could see all my blood vessels on my arms, my chest, my neck, everywhere. Once I started lifting, that turned out to be a good thing.

I found my way to a gym called the Olympus Gym in Falls Church, Virginia. It was a hard-core gym and there were a lot of meatheads hanging out there. Until I walked into that gym, I really had no clue what bodybuilding entailed, or what power lifting was all about. They got me into power lifting and helped me get serious about my body. Once that happened, I really filled out. Lifting—I just took to it like a fish to water. I needed something in my life and that was it.

My body really responded. It just blew up. I'd grown taller for so many years that I never had a chance to fill out. Now that was all I did.

At the time of my senior year in high school, I think I was six five. But I weighed maybe—maybe—two hundred pounds. That's actually very thin for that height. But within a short time of training, I probably put on a good fifty pounds of solid weight.

The people at the gym offered me a job and I grabbed it. It was my first real job out of high school. I worked at the front desk. People would come in and I would show them how to use the machines, the weights, whatever they were working with. I'd do some other odd jobs, helping out here and there. Nowadays, most people working with customers in a gym have to be certified, but back then it wasn't such a big deal. You just had to know what you were doing.

GLENDA

Weight lifting and my job at the gym helped me turn things around in my life. It was like therapy for me, letting me work out my aggressions and also giving me a place to belong. But the real catalyst was the birth of my

Keilani is almost four here.

daughter, Keilani. I realized I had to be a father, I had to provide for her. I started working as a bouncer and picking up whatever income I could.

And I loved that girl. I still do. I love both my girls.

I started going out with their mom, Glenda, somewhere toward the latter half of 1989. I'd recently broken up with the girl who'd been my steady girlfriend for many years. I had no real direction and a lot of the people who knew me, including the family I was staying with, were fed up with me. They thought I was a bum and not doing anything with my life. They were getting ready to throw me out, that's how disgusted they were.

I'd been going to school with Glenda but didn't really know her that well. We started dating that summer. She had a steady job and was still living with her family. When the family I'd been staying with finally got tired of me, Glenda gave me a place to stay and helped me out of that bad situation. I became really dependent on her.

We were together for what seemed like all of two weeks when she got pregnant. And I don't know, it's been a nightmare ever since. I can't even tell you half the stuff she's done. She's made my life more than a living hell.

THE GOOD STUFF: MY KIDS

We got married. Things weren't completely horrible at first. Glenda kept her job. I started working more at the gym and later on got jobs as a bouncer at bars. A lot of times during the day I'd be home watching the baby. It was great. I would put my daughter in the stroller and take her into the gym with me. It'd be like five in the morning, and we'd be working out together.

My second daughter, Athena, was born about two years later. By that time there was really no hope for the marriage.

What happened?

Glenda does things that end up being very destructive to everyone around her. There's no other way to put it. My daughters are the only good thing that came out of that relationship; there's no doubt about that.

Years after we divorced, things got so bad with my ex-wife that I ended up being awarded custody of my girls. It took a long court struggle;

Athena.

I'll talk about it later. But I don't want there to be any doubt about one thing: I've never regretted having my kids. I've really struggled to stay in their lives at different times. I've had a rocky relationship with my older daughter over the past few years, but I've never regretted having her or fighting for her and her sister, even though I don't consider their mother a significant part of my life.

BOUNCING

When I first started working as a bouncer, it looked like easy money. I had a lot of friends who were doing it. It was kind of a cool job to go and stand in a club or a bar and look big. Every so often you'd throw people out. It wasn't very hard work but you'd get paid decently for it. I could work at night, make a few bucks, and then go to the gym during the day. Sometimes I'd get off work and go right to the gym and work out. This would be three or four in the morning, and because the owner had given me a key, I'd have the run of the place.

Checking IDs and looking tough wasn't the only thing I did. Over the years, I had to put the hurt on a lot of people. Professionally, of course.

My first really big job was at a pretty popular bar called Lulu's. A friend of mine named Chris Meighan got a job there as the club manager. I was working at another club, but he offered me a sweet deal to come over and be a bouncer for him. I can't remember how much money it was at the time, but it was really good. They had a restaurant connected to the bar, so there was free food, too. The hours were good, the pay was good, and the people I worked with were good.

Most of the staff there were Sig Eps—members of the Sigma Phi Epsilon fraternity—who had gone to Radford University in Virginia and knew Chris. As a matter of fact, I'd go down to party at the fraternity every so often. Another friend of ours, Mike Connor, would take me along. He was a Sig Ep and also a bodybuilder, a typical meathead.

Not really, though. Because he was mathematically inclined, making him an intellectual meathead. But a great guy and a great partier.

The parties always seemed to end up with drunken fights. One night

I had to haul ass because I got pretty drunk and got into a bad fight. I thought I was going to be arrested. I never found out if I did serious damage to this one kid, but I clocked him and knocked him out. I'm pretty sure I broke his jaw.

Lulu's was very big not only with the college crowd but with the military crowd as well. Now, those two groups don't really mix that well to begin with, so you throw some alcohol into the mix and there can be more than a few problems.

We probably had the biggest bouncing staff in the city, both in numbers and size—a real bunch of meatheads, and I say that with affection. We were constantly tossing people out the door, trying to head off trouble. I've worked at clubs where all the bouncers were just straight thugs. A lot of these guys would pick fights with people just so they could throw them out. Worse: they'd throw them out the back and then rob them. But that wasn't the case at Lulu's. The bouncers—we weren't politically correct enough to call ourselves "security"—really tried to be peacemakers and do a professional job. The cops, though, had a lot of personal problems with the bouncing staff, and they were always looking to arrest somebody. Maybe we were tossing their friends out, whatever. And I have to confess, we weren't the most humble guys about it.

I got arrested a few times while I was working there because of some of the fights I got into with people I had to toss. It's funny: cops come in and look at you and look at the guy on the ground, and if you're a foot or so taller than the other guy, you're in for it. And there are few people who aren't smaller than me.

"There's no way that that guy started a fight with you, no way," a cop would tell me, when of course he had. You have to take into consideration that drunk people will do anything. They get their beer muscles and they pick a fight with the biggest guy in the place.

When that happens, it's not my fault they end up lying on the ground.

I was working at a club near Fifth and K Streets—not Lulu's—at a time when things were getting bad with gangs. We started bringing guns to work for protection, even though we weren't licensed to carry them.

One night, there was a shooting out in the street. I ran out there with my friend Imani Lee. Things got hot and Imani started shooting. He wasn't holding his gun in typical shooting stance. He had it tilted sideways, the way you see in movies, even though it's absolutely the wrong way to fire.

I started laughing. Not very appropriate, but that's what I did.

Fortunately, he didn't hit anyone.

But one of our close friends ended up getting arrested that night. One of the gangbangers went up and told the cops that he had a gun. We had already told him to get rid of it, but he refused. Then the cops came over and he was patted down.

He spent months in a D.C. jail, which is a fucking brutal place.

SHOD FOOT

There was one other situation in particular I remember, probably the worst incident while I was bouncing. A couple of guys were beating up one of our bouncers outside the club where I was working. I came out and pretty much handed them both their asses. But then I went a little bit overboard. After I knocked them both to the ground, I kicked each one of them in the head. They ended up on the ground with their eyes rolling to the back of their heads.

Somebody called an ambulance and the police. I was shitting myself that one of them was going to die. I was arrested and charged with felony assault with a deadly weapon, namely my feet. I believe the charge is officially called "assault: dangerous weapon (shod foot)"; it's issued in cases where a person uses his or her foot in a shoe or a boot to kick or somehow injure someone. Your foot and boot are literally considered dangerous weapons, just like a knife or a gun or a baseball bat.

They ended up dropping the charges. I believe they did that once they interviewed everyone and found out that the guys had started with one of our bouncers and I was just coming to his rescue. In any event, the district attorney didn't have a clear-cut case. But I think that the two guys did bring a civil suit against the bar. I'm not sure whether they won or got a settlement or what, but I do know I lost my job right after that.

CONVICTED OF ASSAULT

One other fight at Lulu's got me into pretty serious trouble. In fact, it ended up with me going on trial for assault.

This frigging asshole was giving Marianne, one of our bartenders, a hard time. He was calling her a bitch and shit like that. I wouldn't have liked that under any circumstances, but it just so happened that she was my girlfriend at the time. So I came up to him and said something to him along the lines of "Call her a bitch again and I'll rip your head off."

Well, he got smart with me, so I dragged him out through the club. I made sure his head met a couple of brick walls on the way out. It was one of those personal things, because he was giving my girlfriend a hard time. So I was a little rough on him and cut his head all up.

So. The police came. I was arrested. I went to court and lost. The jury found me guilty of misdemeanor assault. I was sentenced to probation for a year and began checking in with a probation officer. But the case was soon overturned. It had something to do with the way the judge had instructed the jury; I'm no lawyer, but I guess the appeals court thought the judge had somehow said the wrong thing and in effect directed the jury to find me guilty. Whatever it was, once it was overturned I wasn't retried, and it was erased from my record.

Having worked at Lulu's was like coming out of college with a degree from Harvard Business School, so even though I was let go, I found it pretty easy to get jobs. As I got a little older, into my twenties, I lost the chip on my shoulder and took things a little more maturely. I realized I shouldn't be a jerk-off. I let my size do the talking, not my fists.

After a while, I made a name for myself and started working at better places, more high-end clubs. I began making a lot better money. And I discovered that there are places where people do actually come to have a good time and dance, not get drunk and fight.

At the classier places, bouncing was a lot easier. It was a cake job. I started working with a group of promoters. We'd go to different clubs. All I had to do was show up, stand there, and look big and I'd get paid two or three hundred bucks a night.

About the worst thing that would happen at a club like that was finding people having sex somewhere inside. I'd have to tell them to break it up, get their clothes back on or get zipped up or whatever.

"I realize you guys are drunk and in love," I'd say, "but go out to the car or get a room or something."

I hated to break things up, but I had to.

Every so often, I'd have a brush with a celebrity. Billy Idol came into one of our clubs one night, and they asked me to look after him. So I watched his back. It was no big deal. Billy stood there at the bar and drank and I stood by him and looked big. Nobody bugged him.

We had some other celebrities from time to time. Marky Mark came in, Mark Wahlberg. I'd look after the guy, keep everything cool. It wasn't really a big deal, but the pay was pretty good.

I did a little bodyguarding as well. I bodyguarded for Jamie Foxx and even Michael Moore. Moore came into D.C. to do a documentary, and I was hired to follow him around all day. That was a pretty cool job.

IMANI

I made some good friends while I was bouncing, and a few of them have stayed close. One's Imani Lee, still one of my best friends in the world.

If he wanted to transition into wrestling, he could have at any given time. He's got about a million times more charisma than I do. He's also huge. Right now, he fights for K-1—a mixed martial arts promotion. I keep telling him he ought to go into wrestling.

For a while we went everywhere together, did everything together. We've lifeguarded, bounced, and survived some pretty violent situations together. We watched each other's backs when the shit was flying.

There was this one situation at a bar where there had recently been a shootout inside the club, and we had to try and keep the peace. The place was owned by a friend of ours in D.C., and not the good part of D.C. either. We'd always had some problems with gangs down there, and we nearly got caught in the middle when two different factions decided that they were going to war, and the club was going to be the battleground. It got to the point where we had to wear guns to work, which as a general rule a bouncer won't do.

Imani and I were right there together. One night when things got crazy we had to go outside, literally back to back, and just sweat out the situation. Luckily, things came out all right, but there easily could have been a tragedy. Death was definitely in the air that night.

You go through something like that with somebody, you're going to be tight with them the rest of your life. I guess that's the closest to having a war buddy that someone like me, who's never been in the military, will ever have.

LIFEGUARDING

Another of my jobs at that time was lifeguarding.

Imani and I worked together for a company in the Alexandria, Virginia, area and we were probably the biggest lifeguards those pools had ever seen. The management would have us work the pools in the troubled neighborhoods because there'd be no problems when we were there.

It was at one of these pools that I met another one of my closest friends, Chris Smith. I call him my little brother and he calls me his big brother.

These days, Chris owns his own small business, but when I first met him fifteen years ago, he was a real hell-raiser, nothing but a punk. Chris was about fourteen or fifteen then. He was a white kid but he grew up in an all-black neighborhood. He was raised by a single mom who did all she could to keep him in check, but she must have had her hands full. He had all the potential to be a serious gangbanger.

The first time I ever met him, he started talking shit to me at the pool. I was probably about 325 pounds at the time, and he was a squirt, but that didn't stop him from firing off his mouth.

"Listen, you little fucker," I told him. "Watch your mouth or I'm going to take you in the back, spit on your ass, and prison-fuck you."

He immediately shut up and gave me his respect from that day on.

I realize that wasn't exactly politically correct, and these days it might

Chris Smith with Angie and my mom.

get a lifeguard fired. But we needed order at that pool for the safety of the kids there, and we got it.

Soon after that, Chris and I became great friends. A few years later he got a job as a butcher at a big grocery store chain. It was a time when I was struggling, and he would always manage to find me discounted meat, like really good steaks for two bucks. Since then, he's gone on to start a trucking business and do really well for himself. I was lucky enough to be in a position to help him invest in it; it was one of those things that I wouldn't have been able to do if I hadn't been in wrestling. He's very hardworking, very driven. He's one of the hardest-working people I've ever known. If I could choose brothers, he'd be one.

BODYBUILDING

I was still doing a lot of weight lifting and hanging out in the gym while I was a bouncer. I worked at a number of gyms on and off for years. As my body built up, I started thinking about competing.

The bodybuilders were my heroes at the time. I looked up to them and admired them. They worked hard and were able to make their bodies look extremely powerful. And since all the guys around the gym were competing, I thought I should too. It looked like that's what you did. Lift weights, bodybuild, and compete.

I don't completely remember my first bodybuilding contest. I think I was still a teenager, actually. One thing I do remember is that most of the guys backstage were pretty much arrogant pricks. I didn't like the atmosphere. But I kept at it for years, because I really wanted to get big physically.

The truth is, I never really liked the competitive aspect of bodybuilding, the part where you were being judged against somebody else. I liked the performing part. I didn't mind being up there and posing. I thought it was pretty cool. But the guys around you—arrogant pricks.

THEY JUST WALKED ON BY

I competed in three big bodybuilding contests. The first was Teenage Virginia State. Then I did the Southern States two years in a row, I believe in 1995 and 1996. The '96 contest was my last one and I was really in good shape. But it left me with a bitter taste about bodybuilding.

I'd finished in sixth place as a heavyweight in the Southern States competition in 1995. That sounds good, but the truth is I really got my ass handed to me. It was kind of a humble check, because I went in thinking I was going to go in there and kick everybody else's butt. I was a really big kid, and I really thought I was going to do well.

Didn't work out that way.

I learned from that. I came in the next year and I was so much better.

I'm 330 pounds here.

I'd improved a lot, and this time not only did I really think I was going to win it, I probably had a valid shot at it. I had a good look and with the experience of the year before, I knew what I had to do.

But it was right around then that I had started using diuretics, and whether it was because I had taken too many or I had some sort of other problem that I've never figured out, I ended up cramping up so bad just before the contest began that I wasn't able to line up and go onstage. I literally fell on the ground, writhing in pain. I'm not kidding. I was all seized up, rolling in agony.

All of the heavyweights lined up right in front of me and walked out onstage and nobody ever once said, "Hey, are you okay? What's wrong?" They just walked on by and left me.

When I didn't come out onstage, my girlfriend Marianne ran back to see what was going on. I was lying there on the ground, totally cramped up. She had to drag me out of the locker room and help me recover. If it wasn't for her, I'd probably still be there. None of the other competitors would have lifted a finger for me, and I don't know where the organizers were.

That was it. I was done with bodybuilding.

I thought to myself, This is ridiculous. I'm killing myself for nothing, for a plastic trophy and people who don't give a shit about me. I realized the other bodybuilders were probably glad to see me lying on the ground. I'm sure they thought, "Great. Now I don't have to compete against him."

So that was it.

MARIANNE

I've mentioned Marianne before without really introducing her.

She and I started going out together sometime in 1991, I think, when we were both still working at Lulu's, me as a bouncer and she as a bartender. She was really hot. Extremely hot. We kind of hit it off right away. In one way, we were opposites: she was a big-time flirt, and I was real quiet. But it was an extremely easy fit. She started helping me out after I split with my first wife, Glenda. We started seeing each other and things just seemed to take off.

I was with her for six years. The funny thing is, I didn't want to get married to her. I didn't think she was the right woman for me to get married to. And I didn't think I was the right guy for her to marry.

She wanted to get married. I think she liked the idea of being married more than she wanted to marry me, but the way it worked out, she wanted us to get married and I put it off.

Her dad hated me. He'd say things to her like, "Don't you want somebody with goals, with suits in their closet?" Her mom wasn't that keen on me either.

But she wanted a commitment. So what did I do? Instead of asking her to marry me, I went out and had her name tattooed on my shoulder.

It would only be a year before I had it covered.

ANGIE

I was working out at a Gold's Gym in Alexandria, Virginia. I noticed this woman, a lot younger than me, working out and thought, Wow, she's drop-dead gorgeous. She stood out right away. Her face was so amazing, exotic, I couldn't take my eyes off it. Her hair was Halle Berry short, which was a real turn-on. She also had this tattoo on her shoulder. Nowadays it seems like every woman has a tattoo, but in those days it wasn't as common, and it was another thing that made her stand out.

She always wore a shirt wrapped around her waist, covering her butt. That drove me crazy—I always wanted to check out her butt but she had a shirt wrapped around it. I was extremely attracted to her but she was a lot younger than me and her friends were younger, so I didn't introduce myself or anything. Plus I was pretty seriously involved with Marianne.

The woman's name was Angie. A group of us from the gym were all going to the Arnold Schwarzenegger Classic, the annual fitness and bodybuilding competition. My friend Ray mentioned that she was going to go and also told me that she had this real thing for me. Which really took me by surprise. At that point, I was terrified of talking to women really, but I went up to her and said something like, "I hear you're going to the Classic with us."

When she tells that story, she says that she didn't hear anything I said. She was just so

My first date with Angie.

shocked that I was talking to her that she just stood there and nodded her head.

The first night we went out, I invited her to go to the club I was working at. It was really just a friendship thing still. We hadn't messed around or anything. I invited her to go to the club and she agreed to meet me at my apartment. She thought there were going to be a bunch of people there, and when there weren't, she was very uncomfortable. She barely said two words to me. Then, to make things worse—though I didn't mean to— I asked her to take off her shoe so I could see her foot.

What had happened was this. I'd told my friend Imani, the guy I bounced with, that I'd met this beautiful girl who was just totally perfect. But Imani had this thing with women's feet. He wouldn't date a woman with jacked-up feet. As far as he was concerned, no woman was beautiful if there was something wrong with her toes. Angie had told me that she had been a dancer, and when I mentioned this to Imani he told me to check out her feet. "Make sure she has decent feet," he said.

So after she got to my place, I asked her to take off her shoe. I realize now it was a pretty odd thing to say, but that's what I said. She looked at me like she didn't know what was going on—maybe she thought I was really nutty—but she took off her boot and sock anyway. I was pleased to see she did not have hammertoe or dancer's feet. She had beautiful feet and a pedicure to go with it, beautiful red nail polish, which to me proved that she was perfect from head to toe.

Imani met us at my apartment a little while later. Imani is Mr. Personality, and as soon as he got there, they struck up a conversation. To tell you the truth, I was a little disappointed, even upset. She'd hardly talked to me, but here she was talking to my friend. I thought she was really into Imani. Which would have made sense, I guess, because at the time he was single and I wasn't. We went to the club and after she had a few drinks she loosened up a bit and started dancing. If I hadn't been in love with her already, I would have fallen in love with her then. She was an incredible dancer.

Later that night, she confessed she had a thing for me. We had our first kiss and it was absolutely magical.

Things just took off from there. I went home and called my mother and said, "Mom, I just met the girl I'm going to marry."

We started talking on the phone a lot. I was so in love with her. Totally in love.

And, being in love, and being a jerk, I broke Marianne's heart over it in the worst way.

I was living with Marianne and started seeing Angie on the side. I was so smitten with her, so in love with her, that I would tell Marianne that I was going to the store or something, and instead I'd go over to Angie's mom's house, where she was living at the time. Late at night, I'd sneak into her yard and throw rocks at her window. I was like a kid again. I was just so in love with her that I wanted to see her.

One day, Marianne came home from work about four hours early. Angie and I were on the couch, messing around. I heard the keys rattle and jumped up, naked. Angie wasn't quite naked, but she had most of her clothes off.

It really broke Marianne's heart. If I could change anything, take back anything in my life, I'd take back that moment. I wish I could spare her the heartache. She was a really important part of my life for a long time. We were good friends, very close, and she didn't deserve to be treated like that. No matter what my feelings were for anyone else, I should have done things differently.

It's a huge regret. Marianne deserved better.

YOU CAN'T CHOOSE WHO YOU LOVE

After that, Marianne wanted to get away from everything—me especially. So she left the D.C. area. She moved up to Minneapolis, where her father was working as an exec for an airline.

I moved in with Angie for a very short while, but I was heartsick over what had happened. I hated the way things had ended. And I was confused. I'd been with Marianne so long that I didn't know what to do.

I finally decided to split up with Angie and move up to Minneapolis with Marianne for a while. She took me back, but things were definitely not the same. I think she was really just going through the motions.

And I couldn't get Angie out of my mind. I was calling her every day I was up there. I think I was trying to fool myself into thinking I was trying to make things right, but I really wasn't. I couldn't give up Angie. I was completely obsessed with her. I still am, to this day, even though we're not together.

I got a job with the Powerhouse Gym. Marianne was going to school, pulling herself together. She was right not to trust me, I guess. Whatever my intentions were, I wasn't right for her, and however much I wanted to do the right thing or at least make things between us the way they'd been, she sensed it.

Finally, I figured out that I couldn't live without Angie. So I moved back to Virginia and got back together with her. This was in 1998.

I fell so hard for her, nothing else in the world mattered. You know? It's one of those things: you can't choose the one you love.

CHILI DOGS AND ORANGE GATORADE

I got this little studio apartment in Alexandria, Virginia, and started bouncing again.

And seeing Angie. As much as I possibly could, and that wasn't nearly enough. Twenty-four/seven wouldn't have been enough.

I didn't really ask her to marry me. I gave her this half-assed, shitty proposal. I knew I wanted to marry her, spend my whole life with her, but I couldn't bring myself to get down on my knee and do it right. We were talking one day and I just said, out of the blue, "What do you think about you and me getting married?"

She got really excited and said, "Don't kid around. Don't joke."

I said I wasn't kidding. I was nervous, you know, and not very good at sharing my emotions about something as important as that. Maybe I was worried she'd say no. I sure wasn't kidding.

She said yes right away.

I think that might have been a Friday or a Saturday. We went and got married on a Monday. We just went to the courthouse in jeans. Angie bought us a pair of silver wedding rings. They were thin and simple, all we could afford. Mine didn't even fit. When we got to the part in the ceremony where you put the ring on your spouse's finger, she had to settle for jamming mine only halfway up.

We left the courtroom and went over to the motor vehicle department to get her license changed so her new name would appear on it. I think they weren't supposed to do it right away for some reason. But the clerk felt so bad because Angie was so excited, so happy about being married, that she did it for us. That was the only wedding photo we had, Angie's picture on her license. I still smile, thinking about that.

There was a hot dog stand down near the courthouse. So we got chili dogs and orange Gatorade. That was our wedding feast. On every anniversary, that's what we would eat, chili dogs and orange Gatorade.

We were broke. We lived in a tiny apartment. We had no furniture to speak of. We had a bed and a TV, but nothing to put the TV on.

But man, were we in love.

WRESTLING

It was during the short time that I was up in Minneapolis that I became interested in pro wrestling in a serious way.

Sometime around then I started watching the shows, which I hadn't really done since I was a kid. I loved DX, D-Generation X. I was a big fan of Shawn Michaels and the other guys in that stable. And Goldberg. I've always been partial to the big wrestlers, large guys who could just dominate an opponent. And then there was The Rock and Stone Cold Steve Austin. How could you not love those guys, especially Stone Cold? I just loved his fuck-you attitude. Little by little, watching all those guys, I started to think about what I might do if I were a wrestler.

Curt Hennig, whom I'd admired for a long time, and the original Animal, Joseph Laurinaitis, both used to train at the gym I worked out at, which was called The Gym, over in Plymouth, Minnesota. In fact, J. R. Bonus, the owner of the Powerhouse Gym—which was in Roseville, another suburb of Minneapolis—had wrestled for a short time in the American Wrestling Association, or AWA, which used to be based in Minneapolis and was one of the great old wrestling franchises in its day.

I mentioned Curt Hennig and his career earlier. As I said, injuries shortened his time with the company, but he was still working out and in good shape when I met him in the gym around 1997 or 1998.

Like Hennig, Laurinaitis was also originally from Minneapolis. He began wrestling as the Road Warrior in what was then Georgia Championship Wrestling back in 1982, but it wasn't until the following year when he joined with Hawk—Michael Hegstrand—that he started getting some real heat in the profession as a member of the Road Warriors. At that point, Laurinaitis became known as Animal. He and Hawk wrestled in Japan and for the old NWA before coming over to World Wrestling Federation, as WWE was called at the time.

They would come into the gym and work out and were very encouraging to me. They thought I had a good look and suggested that I might be interested in wrestling.

This was at the height of the competition between World Championship Wrestling and World Wrestling Federation, the so-called Monday Night Wars which pitted WWE's *Raw* against WCW's *Nitro*. Wrestling boomed incredibly in the 1980s and 1990s. The first *WrestleMania*s were cultural phenomena, bigger than anything the sport had ever seen. They were as big as the Super Bowl and twice as fancy. The competition from WCW in the late nineties made pro wrestling even bigger. The two companies went head to head for a while, and it seemed like everyone in the country was into wrestling. These were the days of D-Generation X, the New World Order, Hulk Hogan's monster turn to "cool" bad-ass heel. Wrestling wasn't just big, it was titanic.

A lot of bodybuilders looked at it as something they wanted to do. Most of them, I have to say, thought it would be easy.

For some reason, WCW decided to hold open tryouts around that time. They were advertised on TV. It kind of sparked my interest, and when I got back to Virginia, I decided to take a shot.

I still really didn't know what the hell I was going to do with myself. I thought I looked the part, people had told me I could do it, and so I said, "Hey, I can be a professional wrestler." I really had no fucking clue what I was in for.

I'M A DYING COCKROACH

The tryouts were held at the Power Plant, which was WCW's training facility at the time in Atlanta. I went down with a buddy of mine, Lance Treadway. Lance was just about the same size as me; I was about 340, Lance was about 320. We completely dwarfed every other guy trying out in the class. I thought we had pro wrestler written all over us.

But the lead trainer didn't.

They called him Sarge. He'd wrestled in the mid 1990s as Buddy Lee Parker and I believe his real name was Dwayne Bruce. I think he was five six. Maybe. He was a little midget. He really was. He looked like a little fire hydrant, a jacked-up fire hydrant with stubby legs.

We got out there and he jumped right in our faces and started running us into the ground. He started with free squats, which are your very basic squats with no weights. He was relentless. He put a bucket under our ass, and he made sure our butts touched the bucket every time we squatted.

Now, you have to understand, we're big guys, and after a while, those squats were literally killing us. We couldn't breathe and our legs were water. The guys behind us, they were 170 pounds, 180 pounds, and they were doing half squats and laughing at us.

Sarge worked us to the point where my buddy's nose just exploded. He started bleeding all over the place.

Me, I began puking on the floor. But I did keep going.

Sarge just kept running us into the fucking ground, with these squats and other calisthenics. I was doing them right in my puke. Then he told us to lie on our backs.

Except that wasn't good enough.

"Scream 'I'm a dying cockroach,'" he told me. "Scream 'I'm a dying cockroach.'"

Doing that—yelling anything—takes what little breath you have away. But I did it.

We were starting to get really pissed now. Lance was really mad. I think he bumped some guy who got a little too close to him. It wasn't a gentle bump, either.

Sarge kept dumping on us. I think he had the biggest Napoleon complex of all time. He was determined to run us into the ground and prove that he was better.

Finally, when we were completely exhausted but somehow still alive, he came up to us.

"Forget it," he told us. "You guys are out of here. You're done. You'll never be professional wrestlers. You guys don't have the fucking heart. Get out of my class."

So we left.

HEARTBROKEN

It makes you think.

I had this guy who never amounted to anything tell me I would never be a professional wrestler, that I didn't have what it takes. And a few years later, I was headlining *WrestleMania*. What does that tell you?

I wonder how much talent he chased out of there. The goddamn WCW went under not too much longer after that. Maybe there's a connection.

In my opinion, Lance had a lot more potential than I ever had. Except for his nose. But Sarge and the experience at the Power Plant stifled Lance's wrestling ambitions for a long time. He still has a dream, believe it or not, of being a pro wrestler, but he hasn't made it yet.

Hey, Sarge, if you're reading this—I think about you every day, you fuckin' piece of shit.

Yeah. You're a fuckin' piece of shit.

On the one hand, though, maybe Sarge did help me, because he pissed me off enough to say, "Fuck, I'm going to make it."

On the other hand, that sure wasn't what he was trying to do. He was trying to humiliate us, and he pretty well did that.

On that day, when I went home, I wasn't feeling like I was going to show him up or prove I could make it in WCW's rival or any other wrestling franchise. All I was really feeling was heartbroken.

SOMEWHERE IN ILLINOIS

More nights than not, I'm the last one out of the locker room. Which is a pain for the security guys, because they can't move on until I'm out of the building.

They're patient tonight. By the time I'm done, the truck has already been packed and is heading up toward Urbana, Illinois, and tomorrow's show. It's past midnight; they have a couple of hours of driving ahead of them.

So do I.

It's started to snow and the Lincoln is covered with a light frost. I brush it off and get into the car. I'm real lucky tonight—not only did a friend of mine start it up for me so it's nice and warm when I get in, but none of the boys played with the seat or the radio. A lot of nights I get into the car and my knees are slammed against the steering wheel and country music is blasting in my ears.

I like all kinds of music, but not that. Not at one in the morning.

Or is it two?

The GPS system gives me directions and I head out of the

parking lot toward the highway. Sixty seconds later, I'm stuck in a back alley behind a utility building, squeezed tight against a fence and a stack of cement blocks.

I can see the highway, at least. I back out, fishtail around and ignore the one-way signs, and finally find the road.

Most weeks, our shows are at night, and I can sleep late the next day. But tomorrow is Super Bowl Sunday. To make it easy for people to see the game after our show, we're starting early, at one o'clock in the afternoon. Because of that, I had to change around my hotel reservations. I know from experience it will be best to get up to Urbana first and then sleep; the hotel is only a mile or so from the arena, and even if I get to bed late it'll be easier to get up in the morning and get there on time. But it means driving when I'm exhausted, at the end of a long day.

I break the long, post-midnight run from Carbondale with a stop at a Denny's somewhere in the dark Illinois countryside. A young waitress who says she's just working the midnight shift to bring home a little extra money for her family shows me to a table in the back. She looks at me kind of funny as she hands over the menu.

"Anyone ever tell you that you look like Batista?" she asks, ducking her head a little bit as if she's trying to poke her eyes under the brim of the cap I've pulled low over my face.

"Man, I am so tired of hearing that," I say. Partly that's a joke, and partly that's a plea to get away unrecognized.

She seems to think I'm serious and goes away. Truth is, with my cap and street clothes and heavy winter coat, I don't really look like the World Heavyweight Champion who was strutting into the ring just a few hours ago—at least I don't think I do.

But the fans know. It's dumbfounding—and humbling—but they sure do know. It turns out that the waitress really did know but was trying to be polite.

The restaurant manager comes over with my iced tea a short while later. "We do know who you are," she tells me. "But we want to respect your privacy."

Fair enough. I appreciate that.

While I'm waiting for my food, I try to call home to see how my daughter did on a test she was going to take today. I have some other calls I'm supposed to return, too, and even though it's ridiculously late I take a stab at it. But one by one people start losing their shyness and come over to see me. There's a little girl who's crying she's so excited about getting an autograph, and then a waiter comes to talk about how his little brother would really be amazed to get an autograph.

Once you've been on TV, people want your autograph. Some fans are really cool about it, waiting until I'm done eating or whatever and asking very politely. Others, a few, can get pretty obnoxious. A few think that the price of a ticket or just turning on the TV entitles them to every part of your personal life. And since you've given up your personal life, they can have an autograph any time they want it, even if you're on the phone or eating—or trying to do both at the same time.

Those are the extremist fans, though. Not everybody's like that. A lot of people are really pretty polite. And some are so nervous, they don't even realize they're being rude.

Tonight, I end up posing for photos with the whole staff. They're so jittery they have trouble with the camera, and it's quite a while before I'm back on the road.

When you're tired and hungry, the attention can be a bit of a strain. But the truth is, I am grateful for my career and I understand what the fans are looking for. They want to connect with the good guy, have a hero in their lives who struggles against all the bad shit that happens to them in this world—a crappy day at the office, tough times at home. It's all stuff I went through, and still do.

Outside, the snow has stopped. I gas up the car at an all-night gas station nearby and get back on the road . . .

Three

DUES

In 1999, I turned thirty years old.

In a lot of professions, that's nothing. If you're a CPA, a lawyer, a teacher, a businessman, you're really just getting started at thirty. You can look forward to another thirty-five or forty, maybe even fifty years in your career.

But in wrestling, thirty is damn old. And it's one thing if you're thirty and you're in the prime of your career. If you're thirty and you haven't hit the big time, it's pretty ridiculous to think that you're going to go anywhere. A lot of wrestlers have to hang up their gear by the time they reach their midthirties. Their bodies just won't do what needs to be done.

A guy like Ric Flair is an obvious exception—he just keeps going and going—but even Ric was a champion at age thirty.

Me?

I wasn't even in the ring yet.

CRUSHED

I really had my heart set on wrestling. Despite my fiasco at the Power Plant and Sarge's bullshit pronouncement that I didn't have what it takes to be a wrestler, I wanted it in the worst way.

Most bodybuilders think to themselves that they can become a pro wrestler, but most who try to do it find out it's a lot harder than they think. Instead of trying to change their way of life to make it, they give up.

I didn't do that. I pursued it with everything I had. It was really out of passion and desperation.

I say desperation because I really was desperate. I didn't know, I didn't want, to do anything else. It was all or nothing.

It had taken me forever to figure out what I wanted in life. I'd drifted into bouncing and working in gyms, not really with much of a plan. It was good work and I liked it. I even got paid pretty well at times. But when I started taking an interest in wrestling, it was different. There was a real passion there.

I'm not going to compare it to love. Love is a different thing, something between people. You know that and I know that. But I really felt a deep desire to make wrestling my life. I started watching the shows a lot and thinking of myself as a wrestler, figuring out what I would do. I was really into it. Every other possibility in life suddenly closed off. That was what I wanted.

Being told that I didn't have what it took, that I would never be a wrestler, crushed me.

For two or three days. Then I started making phone calls.

"YOU SERIOUS, SON?"

One of my calls was to World Wrestling Federation. I was just a voice over the phone to them, but whoever answered initially passed me along to someone. I don't remember who, but I do remember what he said:

You serious, son?

I said I sure was. He recommended that I go to wrestling school first to learn the basics, and told me about the Wild Samoan Training Center in Allentown, Pennsylvania. He may also have mentioned that I could talk to Jim Cornette, who was helping spot young talent, the next time WWE came to town.

It just so happened that World Wrestling Federation was coming into town for a house show at the MCI Center in D.C. right around that time. So I went down there and went up to someone and asked if I could speak to Jim Cornette.

I'll take a little time out here to mention Jim Cornette's background. A lot of his two decades or so in the business has been spent helping develop new talent and getting guys ready for WWE. He's also done booking and on-camera work, been a promoter, and most recently was with TNA Wrestling. Some fans might remember that he started Smoky Mountain Wrestling in the early nineties. By the time I heard about him, he was with the company, helping develop new faces. I ended up training under him a year later or so at Ohio Valley Wrestling, or OVW.

So anyway, I went down to the arena beforehand and just walked in. Nobody ever said anything to me. I was there for a little bit. One of the promoters at the time, Doug Sharfsburg, came up to me and asked me what I was doing.

"I'm looking for Jim Cornette," I told him. "I was told I could meet him here."

"What do you need him for?"

"I was trying to get a job, and—"

"Security!"

Doug called security on me, and before I could get much of an explanation out of my mouth, I was thrown out of the building.

Nobody was going to make this easy for me.

That's me with Afa.

AFA

Doug was just doing his job. A couple of years after that, when I was with WWE, we were doing a house show at MCI and I ran into him. I reminded him of that night.

"Oh my God, was that you?" he said.

He felt so bad that from that day on, whatever I asked Doug for, tickets, whatever, he's given me. He's probably apologized a hundred times. But he thought I was just some guy who wasn't supposed to be back there. And at the time, I guess I wasn't.

Where I did belong was in wrestling school, the Wild Samoan Training Center, to be exact. Taking lessons from the Wild Samoan himself, Afa Anoa'i.

Afa is a legend in the pro wrestling world, but not too many people know that he joined the U.S. Marines when he was only seventeen. This was during the Vietnam era, when most people thought joining the military wasn't really the coolest or smartest thing you could do. He came out of the service and began wrestling during the 1970s.

He was pretty successful, but it wasn't until after he taught his brother Sika to wrestle that he really catapulted to fame. In the 1980s, Afa and Sika formed the Wild Samoans tag team. I'm not sure how many championships they won altogether, but I know they had the World Wrestling Federation titles at least three times.

Since he's retired, Afa has become pretty well known in the industry as a trainer. There's a whole flock of Samoans related to Afa who found their way into the sport because of him. Just in his family, there's an all-star cast of guys he's helped: Samu (his son), Rikishi and Yokozuna (his nephews), and Umaga.

Afa's school is located in Allentown, Pennsylvania. There's a lot of wrestling history in that area; Vince McMahon's father used to do television tapings there before World Wrestling Federation expanded into a national franchise. It's not so far from New York and other big cities that you can't get there in a few hours, but it's far enough off the beaten track that a young guy can learn the trade without being completely distracted.

MY FRIENDS WERE THERE FOR ME

Like any other school, the Wild Samoan Training Center charges tuition. Not only did I have to come up with that, but I needed money to live on. Angie was working, but she wasn't making all that much money and there was no chance of her supporting both of us.

So I talked to my friends Jonathan Meisner and Richard Salas. Both Jonathan and Richard have been my friends for a long time; even today, they're still two of my very closest friends. I've known Richard since high school, when he and I and his brother Wilbur—another close friend—wrestled together. He's Filipino and we had a little clique going back then. I still kid him because he hooked me up with my first wife—though believe me, I don't hold it against him. I met Jonathan a few years later through Richard, and we've been incredibly close for years and years. He still helps me out. I can't even tell you how much he helps me out. He's my closest friend in the world.

When I went to them and told them what I wanted to do, they put their money where their friendship was. They bankrolled everything for me. It was probably around $150,000 altogether. They never ever once said no; they never even asked when they were going to get the money back. All they said was, "We know you can make it."

Really, they made my dream possible for me. They bankrolled the whole thing. They just did it on friendship. Those are friends. Real friends. I love them both very much.

WHERE HAVE YOU BEEN?

We all went up to Pennsylvania together, my wife, Angie, and Jonathan and Richard, to check out the school.

Afa was there. I recognized him immediately.

And in a way, he recognized me. He came up to me and said, "Where've you been?"

It was like I was the student he'd been looking for his entire life. He treated me like a son right off. Afa, he's a big guy. He's from a family of big guys. But there were no big guys for him to train there. Until I came. I was kind of like his pet project—his little toy.

To this day, I think of Afa as a member of my family. I call him Pops. Anytime Pops calls me up to do an appearance, if my schedule permits, I make it my business to help him out. I've helped him raise money for his charity organization. It's a debt I owe to him as a wrestler, and also as a person. He's really been that good to me. I love him for that.

ALLENTOWN

We moved to Allentown, close to Afa. We packed our stuff in a tiny car—my wife owned a Honda Del Sol. I don't know if you remember the Honda Del Sol, but it was a very small sports car, smaller than today's Civic. You should have seen me in a Honda Del Sol. It was ridiculous.

Anyway, we moved up to Allentown. The training center was in Hazelton, Pennsylvania, which is about forty-five minutes away. For a while, Angie was traveling back to Virginia to work, because it was so hard to find a job up there. We lived in the nicest apartment complex around, but just outside of where we lived, there were a lot of real run-down buildings.

I don't know about now, but at the time unemployment was real bad. Allentown was part of the "rust belt." America's industrial heartland had basically rusted by the late 1990s, as old industries suddenly found they couldn't compete. A lot of jobs were lost when manufacturing started going overseas. Unemployment surged. Whole cities and regions were suddenly poor. You had a lot of social problems; still do.

That pretty much described Allentown when I was there. There wasn't a lot of work, and seeing young teenage girls pushing strollers around was not uncommon.

I actually didn't train with the class much when I was at the school. I was Afa's own little pet project. He and his son worked with me a lot, personally, just one-on-one. Simple things. I learned how to run the ropes, how to take falls. Very, very basic stuff, but I had to learn it all.

There was a gym in town called Phoenix Fitness. I couldn't really afford a gym membership, but one day I went in and, hoping for a cheap rate, introduced myself and told them that I was trying to become a pro wrestler. They actually gave me a free membership for myself and Angie. They felt that I was going to make it as a professional wrestler. I'll never forget their kindness.

I'd never done much cardio work during my weight-lifting years. I started doing it in the ring, trying to get in better shape. That's one reason that throughout those early years I consistently dropped weight. You can look back at the pictures and see me getting progressively leaner.

I did a few matches while I was at the school, but they weren't really matches. I'd go out there and hit the guy with a couple of things and kind of kill him. It'd take about thirty seconds and the match was over; I was out of there. I still had a lot to learn.

THIS GODDAMN ARM

I also had my first injury while I was training with Afa. It was a torn triceps, the same one that's given me problems in WWE. I believe it must go back to a really early injury when I was lifting weights that were way too heavy. At the time, I didn't notice any real problem, but I may have been setting myself up for problems later on. It was one of those things that you don't realize at the time because you're young, full of piss and vinegar. As you start to get older, the stuff starts catching up with you.

Anyway, I was in the ring and I was doing front bump drills: you jump up in the air and land on your stomach. My arm had been bothering me, God, for a couple of years, to the point where I couldn't do bench presses anymore, or even push-ups. I never really knew what was wrong with it, but it hurt like hell if I pushed it.

That day it just snapped. It hurt like hell—and then some. I went to the hospital, and they said, "Oh you just pulled a muscle."

"I don't think so," I said. "It's swelled up twice as big as normal. I don't think that's a swelled muscle."

"Oh, yeah," said one of the doctors. "Just take some Advil and you'll be fine."

Uh-huh.

That same night, my arm swelled up some more. The pain was so bad I had to go to the emergency room. They had MRIs done and we found out it was torn. I had to have surgery to reattach it.

I was out for a few months. Soon after I came back, Afa decided I was ready to move on. He made a phone call to WWE and set up a tryout for me. The next thing I knew I was headed up to WWE headquarters in Connecticut.

AUDITION

I was terrified.

I went up there with a bunch of other guys who were being tested for possible contracts. One had been at WCW for a while. He was very experienced and seeing him try out, doing all these high spots and complicated moves, made me feel like an idiot. I think Tazz was up there, too, working out. He'd just come over from ECW and was in the ring that day, working on some moves. I'll always remember how good he was to me that day, just a real gentleman to me and my wife.

The tryout was completely different from what I'd gone through at WCW. It was very one-on-one, very personal. I got in the ring with Tom Prichard. He knew I really didn't know how to wrestle that much. What he wanted to do, I think, was check out my footwork, see if I had good balance, find out if I was agile.

"We'll just do what you know," he told me, and away we went. We got in the ring and locked up a little bit. I hit the ropes. He had me show him some body slams and stuff like that, did a little bit of chain wrestling, and then I showed him my footwork. Tom wasn't looking to bury me or run me into the ground. He just really wanted to know if I was athletic.

Wrestling is not ballet, it's very physical. But there is a dancelike element to it. You have to have enormous control over your body, how you move. Obviously, the look is important, but if you don't have the athleticism and technique to back that up, you're not going to be any good.

You also need judgment and a kind of restraint. No matter what it looks like, we can't manhandle guys in the ring. A wrestler had to use his strength in a way that not only entertains the crowd, but also protects the guy he's working with. It takes even more strength sometimes not to hurt a guy than to just go ahead and pummel him. And it takes craft and art to make it look good while doing that.

I was always afraid of hurting guys when I was starting out. I didn't want to be overly powerful. That became a problem after a while. Because of the way I look, if I take it easy, really supereasy on a guy, it just looks like shit. The crowd is expecting me to be this big killer, which is basically the way I wrestle. If I lie back, that makes whoever I'm wrestling against look like a wimp. I have to go at it for real. They have to look good so I look good, and vice versa.

I can brag about one thing: I have never, ever hurt anyone. To me, that means a lot.

I think Tom saw that I understood that part of wrestling, even though I wasn't at the stage where I could do it like an experienced pro could. I'm sure he liked that I was a real big guy but wasn't clumsy on my feet, that I had real good balance and was athletic.

And I also had the look.

Bruce Prichard—Tom's brother, who was in charge of development—walked by the ring while we were working. (Hard-core wrestling fans probably remember Bruce as "Brother Love," the preacher man who helped ignite a number of feuds during the late eighties and the nineties. Brother Love managed Undertaker during the first year or so of 'Taker's career at WWE.) Bruce took one look and kept going. Then he stopped in his tracks, took a hard look up, this time really watching me. I remember that look clearly to this day.

It meant I could make it, if I worked hard enough.

"IF I WERE YOU ..."

Bruce Prichard called me the very next day and said, "We want to offer you a contract."

I told him I'd like some time to think about it.

"Well. This is what it's going to be," he told me. "We're offering you this. You get your foot in the door and if I were you, I'd take it."

So I took it. There was never any question about it, actually.

I was hoping they'd offer me a lucrative contract, but the truth is they didn't. It was $650 a week. It was a yearlong contract, a typical developmental deal.

Well, not typical. When I got out to the training facility, I found out I was the lowest-paid guy down there.

I didn't really care. Like Bruce said, I had my foot in the door. Angie and I packed the car and headed out for Louisville and Ohio Valley Wrestling.

OHIO VALLEY WRESTLING

Ohio Valley Wrestling—or OVW—is one of those regional wrestling franchises that can trace its roots pretty far back in our profession. Most recently, though, it's been known mostly as a development circuit for WWE. Some of the biggest stars in the business right now have come out of OVW. John Cena, Boogeyman, Ken Kennedy, Randy Orton—I can't possibly name all the people who worked at OVW and are now wrestling on *Raw* or *SmackDown!* or ECW.

OVW has a regular wrestling school with different levels of training; the students range from kids who are really just getting a small taste of the business to veterans who've been injured and need to get back into show shape. Just as important from the fan's point of view, though, OVW has a full slate of live matches as well as a television show. The television show is shot in the Davis Arena in Louisville. OVW house shows, which of course aren't televised, are held throughout Kentucky, Indiana, and Ohio.

In a way, OVW works like the minor leagues work for baseball. WWE calls up OVW wrestlers for its own live events from time to time. This gives the people at WWE a chance to look at how the new talent is coming along, and gives young wrestlers a taste of the big time. And OVW wrestlers are all working toward the day when WWE calls and gives them a chance to appear as a regular or semiregular with one of the three "brands."

IN A WAREHOUSE

Angie and I didn't have much when we moved to the Louisville area. We had a futon and our clothes. At first they told us that they were sending us down to Memphis, so we made our plans for Tennessee, but then just a week before, they called and told us things had changed; we were headed for OVW.

Anyway, we got all our shit together and we packed up a U-Haul trailer, attached it to the Honda, and drove out. I remember the first day we pulled in front of the training center, which was across the bridge from Louisville in Jeffersonville, Indiana. Now, I had thought it was going to be a high-tech facility. You know, "WWE TRAINING CENTER!!" A big-lights, latest-technology, top-of-the-industry, nothing-too-good-for-us kind of place.

It was the biggest shit hole on the face of the earth. It looked like a goddamn abandoned warehouse with the windows all knocked out.

I think my wife started to cry. And they weren't tears of joy.

BOOT CAMP

It was tough for Angie at first, moving there. It was tough for me, too, but I was pursuing my dream.

The inside of the training facility was just about as desperate-looking as the outside. There was nothing fancy about this place, believe me. When I got there, we had a ring that was such a piece of shit. If you stood in the middle of it, it would sink down about ten inches. They ended up putting in a new ring only because Big Show, who was a WWE star at the time, injured his knee and came down to OVW to rehab.

Training was like boot camp. Drills, drills, and more drills. God, they'd just drill us to death. Then we'd do matches. I had tons of matches. I even had a few with big names. Every once in a while, we'd have big shows in Louisville. I remember a big match with Kane, and one where Kane and Undertaker tagged against me and DDP—Diamond Dallas Page.

The first guy I did a practice match with was Scotty O—Scott Oberholser. I think he wrestled with WCW and us, but I don't think he ever made it onto TV. The match was god-awful, because I didn't know how to wrestle. The funny thing is, I ran into him recently at a *WrestleMania* and we were both amazed at how far I've come in the last few years. But back then I knew a couple of moves and that was it. And the matches were completely scripted for me, written down on pieces of paper: *get in, lock up, shoot the guy off you, body slam*. I had a lot of matches, but I never really got to work, to really push myself the way a good wrestler has to. All I was taught to do was string a few moves together. They showed me all the moves, but I never felt as if I really got control of them the whole time I was down there. And I think I touched the microphone like once, maybe twice, on the TV shows in two years.

LEVIATHAN

Jim Cornette was a talent developer and part owner at OVW. He created a character for me, Leviathan, which was pretty cool. It was kind of old-school, a little cheesy and hokey, but it was still real cool. I had a lot of fun with it, and a lot of people still remember Leviathan. Every so often, someone even asks me to sign autographs as Leviathan.

I was supposed to be a demon raised from the Ohio River. We actually went down there and shot it on video. It was pitch-black. I got in the water, which of course was freezing. Somebody had told me that there were alligators in the river. Being from the streets, I didn't know much about rivers or alligators, so I believed them. The whole time I was in the river I was shitting myself, I was so afraid that some alligator was going to come up and snatch me.

Synn, my manager, started doing this incantation, saying all this crap that nobody could understand. And I walked out of the water toward this bonfire they had going on the shore and growled like I was Frankenstein or something. There I was: Leviathan was born. Thank God we got it in one take, because I didn't want to go back in—I didn't want to get eaten by alligators.

From then on, I was Leviathan. I was kind of an indestructible monster wrestler, not really human. Week after week, they broke everything imaginable over my head, bricks and chairs, just to show I was invincible. Meanwhile, I'd go home every night with a headache.

But it was really cool. That was my first taste of being on TV, and of course I was wrestling every week. The problem was, the matches I was in were really short. I'd come out and squash whoever I was matched up against. That was the kind of character I was. Who's going to beat a super-human monster?

Leviathan. A good character,
but I wasn't a good wrestler.

The bad part is, I never learned how to work because the matches were over so quick. And the character really didn't have much to say. I looked great—I had the body of a wrestler. But I really didn't know how to use it.

To show you how bad I was: I remember this one match I was having with Kane in some casino. It wasn't for OVW, it was some independent circuit. Kane was wearing a mask at the time, and while we were wrestling, he was laughing under his mask. Really roaring, because I was stinking up the place so bad. There was one point where I was supposed to give a spear. He yelled, "Spear, spear!" So I gave him a half-assed attempt at a spear, but it looked like I just ran up and gave him a big hug. And that's the way the first half of my career was. I looked like a million bucks, but I didn't know how to wrestle and I just stunk.

It wasn't for lack of trying. I didn't know how to make myself better.

I did cardio, tried to drop some weight, even struggled with my asthma. I got into much better shape. But I didn't learn a whole lot of wrestling down there. I learned moves, but even when I left there, I wasn't very good by any means. And I wasn't ready for the spotlight, not by a long shot.

TALKING

One of the problems I had at OVW had nothing to do with wrestling. I'm kind of a quiet guy by nature. Doing interviews wasn't very easy at all. As a matter of fact, later on when I would be interviewed on radio or for some news story or something, a lot of times I would bring my wife. The interviewer would ask the question and I'd have maybe a word or two for them, and that would be it. But my wife could give them a lot more.

Some of my family's friends were kind of surprised when they heard that I was going into wrestling. They wished me well and everything, but they were wondering how I would do when it came to television. They thought I would just be too shy to go on-screen. But I can be the Animal when I'm in character. The Animal may not say much, but he's not shy about being in the ring, or about himself. That was one of the things that

I started to learn at OVW, and later at WWE: how to become the character I was playing on television.

I think on a lot of interviews since I've become famous, just because of the questions I've been asked, I've focused in on a lot of the negatives of Ohio, what I didn't learn, what I failed to figure out. I never really got to speak out about what I did learn. So let me take the time now to focus on a few other things that I did pick up there, and that I am grateful for having been taught.

One thing that I always loved about Jim Cornette is the fact that he's a huge buff of the history of wrestling. He would make us study. We read Lou Thesz's book, *Hooker: An Authentic Wrestler's Adventures Inside the Bizarre World of Professional Wrestling,* to get a feel for the industry, especially as it was during the eighties and early nineties. He gave us another book whose title I don't recall, but which had a lot of information on older wrestlers, guys who had passed away. And we watched shoot interviews with Cowboy Bill Watts. Watts was an old-school wrestler and then wrestling promoter who had a tremendous store of information and stories about wrestling. By "shoot" I mean that his interviews weren't in character; he was telling the viewers a lot about the inner workings of the business.

Jim Cornette really tried to school us on the traditions of sports entertainment. He was really big on making sure we knew our history. I always loved that about Cornette. Danny Davis was the trainer when we were down there. I always liked him, though he always seemed stressed when I was around. He was good to me, though. So was Nick Dinsmore—probably better known to fans as Eugene—who was teaching classes at the time.

I learned a lot at OVW about the responsibilities that come with being a wrestler. Some are pretty simple, like just being on time and doing your job. Simple, but important.

There's a lot more to being a wrestler than just being out there in the ring. I really learned how to be responsible. I really grew up a lot as a person at OVW. Before then, all my jobs were at places where I could more or less do what I wanted. Everybody I worked with or for was always my friend. I could come and go as I pleased.

Jim Cornette.

At OVW, there was more responsibility on my shoulders. I don't want to say it was a huge burden, but there were things I had to do, and I had to do them right. My part in the ring, showing up at appearances, taking time for the fans—these things and more were all part of my responsibilities as a wrestler. I realized this was my one and only shot, and I didn't want to freakin' blow it.

AN ALL-STAR CAST

We had an all-star cast down there. A lot of the guys who were in there around the time that I was moved up and became huge stars. I'm talking about guys like Shelton Benjamin, Randy Orton, Brock Lesnar, Rico Constantino, and John Cena. They were all wrestling at OVW during that time period.

Shelton and I were never superclose, but he's one of those guys I've always liked from day one. He's probably one of the most easygoing guys I've ever met in my life. I don't want to say he's floating through life, but he does seem to just blow in the wind. He's a naturally gifted athlete. It's freaky some of the things he can do.

And every once in a while, he'll just break out into an impersonation of someone and it'll be the funniest freakin' thing. Just crack you up. On the microphone, though, he's so dry. I don't know why that happens.

I'd met Brock up in Minneapolis before either of us was in the business; we'd both trained together in the gym. He was still wrestling for the University of Minnesota, where he won the NCAA championship in 2000 as a heavyweight. Brock is one of the strongest guys I've ever met in my life. He's just a freak of nature—strong and fast and agile. He's unbelievable. His parents are like normal people, but he's just an incredible freak of nature. It's as if a meteorite brought him to earth.

I was disappointed when Brock left WWE. Besides having good technique and wrestling skills, Brock was awesome at psychology, at doing the things you have to do to sell a match. It was too bad—I always thought that if he and I had gotten together, we would have given the fans a great show. It would have been magic, a real battle of the giants.

Randy Orton and me during our OVW days.

Rico—Americco Tomhas Constantino—is an interesting guy. It would take me hours to get you to understand the way Rico is. He's probably one of the most entertaining guys I've ever met. Toward the end of his career, he took a little bit of a surly turn, but back in OVW he was a big cheerleader, real positive and very happy. He was one of the guys who was so proud of being a wrestler. Every so often you'd catch him wearing his OVW belts out in public. He was just so proud of what he did. He's a good guy, one of those people you can trust, which is rare in this business. He and I rode together for a while. He was always wired at the end of the night, so he would do the driving. I will always consider Rico a close friend and someone I can trust.

CENA

Cena is huge now. He just starred in the movie *The Marine*, so he's known to audiences that don't even follow wrestling. He's a WWE Champion and is one of *Raw*'s biggest stars.

Now back when he was at OVW, he was the whitest white kid I had ever met. Somehow he turned himself into a streetwise, thuggish kid. I don't know where that came from. But it worked.

John's impressive on so many levels, it's ridiculous. He's probably one of the smartest guys I ever met. He's got a freaky memory. And he can rap freestyle like crazy. It's just incredible. If you gave him a word, gave him a subject, he could just go rhyming on it, rapping off the top of his head, forever. It's amazing. I've listened to him rap for ten, twenty minutes. Just freestyle rapping about a sign he saw, the trees, whatever. It was pretty entertaining, just amazing.

At first, it didn't have anything to do with his wrestling. It was just a talent he had. Then I think Shane McMahon got wind of it and asked him to do it. From there I think they worked it into his character for him.

Physically, of course, Cena's a specimen. He's a damn freak. He was like that, even down at OVW. He's always been superimpressive.

A STRUGGLE FOR MY WIFE

We didn't really travel in OVW. We'd go do shows in high schools and other spots an hour or an hour and a half away from Louisville, but it wasn't a real taste of life on the road. We always slept in our own beds every night. Which was definitely a good thing for me, family-wise.

I think my wife, Angie, was starting to struggle a little bit with me being in wrestling. From the first day we got together, she was crazy insecure. I don't think there was a time in our marriage when she didn't think that I was cheating on her. The circumstances that we started under probably had something to do with that. But at least at OVW I was able to come home every night, and we spent a lot of time together.

Celebrating Keilani's birthday.

For me, I was having a hard time being away from my kids. I was trying to keep in touch with them, mostly through the phone. Their mom worked for United Airlines at the time, and she had them fly out to see me when she could. I always appreciated that.

Financially, we still struggled a little bit, because I wasn't making much money. But the truth is, things were pretty good. I was home every night, in love with my wife, and she was in love with me. We were together.

I thought it was hard at the time, 'cause it seemed like it was hard going to wrestle every day, then trying to work out, doing a few shows a week. But God, what I would give now to have those easy days back.

BUSTED

The WWE would call us up every once in a while to do dark matches for one of their shows. A dark match is a wrestling contest that is held before the television show itself begins; the fans in the arena see it, but it never goes on the air. Those dark shows gave WWE a chance to see how we were coming along and to judge the audience reaction to us, that sort of thing.

We did this one match in Chicago, I think, where I tagged with Mr. Perfect against Shelton Benjamin and I think Randy Orton. We couldn't find Mr. Perfect before the match. I was a nervous wreck. He showed up literally as we were ready to walk out.

Like I said, I was an emotional wreck. I'm saying, "What are we doing? What are we going to do out there? What are we doing?"

I was used to having everything told to me: do this, this, this, and this. But Mr. Perfect—Curt Hennig—was from the old school.

"Ah, we'll just call it out there," he said, meaning that once we were in the ring, we'd decide the moves that would be made.

I just about freaked out. But of course that was the way we had to do it.

So we were in the ring. I was with Shelton Benjamin and I had no clue what the hell I was doing. But I had to make the call. So I had Shelton give me something really stupid, like an elbow. Which I bumped for, going down on my back. He covered me. So I'm down on the mat, he's covering me, and I'm trying to come up with something to tell him what we're going to do when we get up.

Before I could think of *anything*, I got counted out.

He beat me because of an elbow?

Oh, fuck.

Fuck!

I was freaking out. Mr. Perfect's freaking out. The fans were freaking out. They started booing. And booing. I actually think we did a restart. It didn't matter. I just wanted to die right there.

After the match, I got my stuff, I found my wife.

My first magazine article.

"We gotta get outta here," I told her. "Let's go."

I felt so embarrassed. I didn't want to talk to anyone. I just wanted to leave.

But that would have been too easy.

Angie had been there for a while and was a little tipsy.

Drunk may be a better word.

"How many beers did you have?" I asked her.

"Two?"

"You got six cups in your hand."

"Oh, I'm busted."

My wife had been in the audience drinking beer, having a good ol' time, while I was making an ass of myself in the ring. That wouldn't have been bad at all, except that when we went out to try and find our car, she couldn't remember where she parked it. We couldn't find it. We must have spent like two hours looking for my car.

It's a funny story now, but that night I wasn't laughing.

HURRICANE

Hurricane—Gregory Helms—became a real good friend of mine later on. But the first night I met him, I had had such a fucking awful match. You know it's bad when you go up to gorilla—the ready-room area during a wrestling show, named after famous wrestling commentator and wrestler Gorilla Monsoon—and no one will look at you, not make eye contact or anything. Well, it was one of those nights. I felt so bad and I was sitting down and pouting, just about heartbroken and maybe ready to cry because my match was so bad.

Hurricane walked over to me and he didn't know me from anything, but he was looking out for me. He said, "Man, don't let these guys see you like that. Pick up, put a fake-ass smile on your face, and don't let these guys see you down."

I'll never forget that. He went out of his way to help me out. He's my boy. Even though he is an abrasive dickhead.

There were other times when I was just so embarrassed I left without talking to anyone, not even saying good-bye. I'd get my stuff, grab Angie, stalk back to the car, and get out of there.

DEACON BATISTA

I was at OVW for two years as Leviathan, from 2000 to 2002. I had a shaved head, a big chain around my neck, and black trunks. Whatever was or wasn't happening for me at WWE in those dark shows, I was doing pretty well at OVW. I had the look, and after a while, I became a really big deal there. I won the OVW Heavyweight Championship from Doug Basham, who was wrestling as the Machine.

I was ready to move up, or so I thought. I kept hoping the call would come.

Brock Lesnar had been at OVW around that time. Among other things, he and Shelton Benjamin were the OVW Southern Tag Team champs. Brock had been a star college wrestler before turning pro, he had a real good look, and WWE had very high hopes for him. He was called up and went on *Raw*, I believe in March 2002. Right away, they brought him out as a star.

I thought they'd do the same for me.

Heh.

It was Johnny Ace who finally called me and said they wanted me on *SmackDown!* Johnny Ace's real name is John Laurinaitis; he's head of talent at WWE.

"We're starting you on TV next week," he told me. "So we need you to go out and buy a really nice suit."

He gave me all the other information I needed to know. I was beyond excited. I went out and bought a nice suit, a really nice suit. I spent five hundred bucks, which was a lot of money for us, because I still wasn't making much. But I had the suit tailored and everything. It was perfect.

I showed up in my suit, and whoever I was reporting to said, "Come over here, kid. We need to cut the sleeves off of your suit."

My five-hundred-dollar suit?

"You're fucking kidding me," I said.

"No, come here."

"You're *really* kidding me."

Even here I look confused

They weren't. They cut the sleeves right off. I might just as well have taken out five hundred-dollar bills and set them on fire. At least I would have been warm for a second or two.

Then it got worse.

"Here, strap this thing on," said somebody, holding out this big metal box in front of me. It was like a strongbox. It didn't exactly look like a regular piece of wrestling gear.

"This is what you're doing," said the guy with the box. "This is your character: Deacon Batista."

They put me out in this goofy suit and strapped this goofy box around my neck. They made me look like a cartoon character. I was a bodyguard for the Reverend D-Von. The box was supposed to be his cash box, where he put donations that he would collect from his congregation for his building fund.

I was totally confused. I was wearing a cut-up suit and carrying this dumb cash box around. I could have been anybody, dressed like a goon. They took away my star asset, my body, and I had no idea why.

Now I understand why they did it. They wanted to force me to learn how to work. They were doing it by taking away what I'd always relied on, my body, and forcing me to learn how to work the crowd with other tools. I wasn't ready for the spotlight. Not by a *long* shot. I had dues to pay, and a lot to learn.

And WWE wasn't exactly primed for me, either. D-Von couldn't even pronounce my name right at first. When I came out he called me "Bas-ti-ta" or something like that. They had to voice over it later on before the show aired.

That first show I wasn't in a match. I just came out with D-Von and looked menacing. The first thing I ever did as a wrestling move was clothesline Triple H outside the ring. I knocked the crap out of him. That was my first TV spot ever.

The week after that, I started on live event tours.

At my first house show, I went out and somehow managed to split my pants, from the front top to the back top. I had white underwear on, and black pants, so it was obvious that my pants were split. Bill DeMott—he was wrestling as Hugh Morrus at the time—just started laughing. He made a huge scene out of it. You could hear him throughout the whole place: "Ah, he split his pants. He split his pants."

The whole arena started laughing. I was trying to play this big tough bodyguard, and ten thousand people were laughing at me.

From then on, I wore black underwear.

THE BUILDING FUND

The gimmick with D-Von was pretty funny, and after a while the crowds got really into it. Basically, D-Von was a crooked preacher. So he'd come out with this basket and collect money for his building fund. Well, just before I got there, someone had stolen the money. So enter Deacon Batista, the protector of the building fund—that big metal box with the chain—and the protector of the Reverend D-Von.

The thing was, we'd go out and do a show, and as we walked up to the ring people would wave money at us for the building fund. Of course we'd grab it.

The fans really got into it. As soon as that first person came out with a dollar, everybody else started pulling money out of their pockets. They wanted to be part of the show. Some of this was on television but it was really big at house shows. Guys wanted to be funny, wanted to be big time, so they'd pull out twenties. I think once we even got a hundred-dollar bill.

At night, we were leaving there with two or three hundred extra bucks every night. Which, as far as I could tell, mysteriously vanished. Maybe one of these days I'll check to see if D-Von did build a church after all.

DEVON HUGHES

The Reverend D-Von, of course, was Devon Hughes, who fans may also know as D-Von Dudley. He started wrestling professionally around 1991 and was in the ECW before coming over to WWE. (They were separate companies in those days.) By the time I got there, Devon was a pretty big star and a well-respected veteran. After wrestling with Bubba Ray as the

The Dudleys,
D-Von and
Bubba.

tag team Dudley Boys, he worked the corrupt preacher angle as Reverend D-Von on *SmackDown!* He'd just started doing that when I came on as his bodyguard.

Devon was the guy who broke me in on the road. He was the first guy I drove with consistently. He was a veteran but he really took me under his wing. He looked out for me, making sure I knew the ropes of being on the road. He was really my introduction to a lot of the things about this business that you can't find in a book.

Devon liked to hang out a lot. He was real big on going out and having a few drinks after the shows. I'd always tease him because he drank white Zinfandel wine. A great big muscled-up black dude, and he'd go in and order white Zinfandel, a drink most of us think of as a girl's drink. Now I get ragged on because I always order Malibu.

Devon also showed up with new jewelry every week. We used to always make fun of that, too. We said he had a Mr. T Starter Kit. He had a ring on every finger and about twenty gold chains around his neck.

IN THE EYE

I was nervous as a rookie. Trying to fit in, trying to show the veterans that you belong, can be difficult. It doesn't take much to fuck up.

One of my early matches, we were working against Ron Simmons. I can't remember who he was tagging with. You know, Ron's a huge guy. He's pretty intimidating. And with me just starting out, I didn't want to ruffle any feathers or piss anybody off. Especially not Ron Simmons.

We worked a match with him and I accidentally thumbed him in his eye. I felt my thumb go in at least an inch. Well, maybe not an inch, but it definitely went into his eyeball. He fell out of the ring and he was holding his eye. He was covering it. I'm thinking, Oh God, this guy, he's going to kill me. Here I am with the company only a few weeks, and I already buried myself with a veteran.

After the match we got backstage ahead of him. I told D-Von that Ron was going to kill me. Then Ron came in and I started apologizing all over the place.

"Hey, Ron, I'm so sorry," I told him. "I'm really sorry."

"For what?" he said. His eye was pretty much swelled shut.

"Your eye. I'm sorry I thumbed you."

"My eye?" He tried blinking, but it wouldn't quite open.

"Yeah, really, I'm sorry. I didn't do it on purpose. It was just an accident."

"This?" He made a face and then rubbed it. "Naaahhhh, man, I just have some sweat in my eye."

"I—"

"You didn't do anything, kid. I just got a little sweat in it. Everything's cool. No problem, man."

He tried not selling it, pretending it was okay, but his eye was too swelled to even open right. But there he was, giving me a pass. He must have seen how nervous I was and really just felt sorry for me.

It shows you what a good guy Ron is. He could have easily ripped me apart, in front of everyone, and some veterans might have. But Ron Simmons was the kind of guy who had a lot of class, the kind who knew how to inspire a rookie just by being himself.

Thinking about Ron reminds me of some other friends of mine who really helped me out in the early days. Two I don't want to forget to mention are Tommy Dreamer and Stevie Richards, who were great friends to me. They really encouraged me. Tommy still offers advice from time to time, but I don't see Stevie much these days. Still, I just love them to death. Both of them have been wrestling with our ECW brand lately, and I love to watch their work every chance I get.

A ROOKIE'S MISTAKE

Riding with D-Von, I saw for the first time what it means to be a wrestling star. You go out and girls are throwing themselves at you, and guys are kissing your ass. People are really big fans and will do anything to hang out with you. That was a new world for me. D-Von had been everywhere. The Dudley Boys were a huge deal, really big in the wrestling world. We never went anywhere where they didn't know who D-Von was.

Even though D-Von could start a party just by walking into a place, he was also one of those guys who, no matter where we were or how much time we had, would manage to find a gym and work out. It always amazed me. And he didn't just get in the gym and do a light workout, he busted his ass. He did cardio, a run, a full workout. Then he'd go and do a match.

He also kept the guys off my back a little bit. Pro wrestling can be real competitive. It's a cutthroat business. Certain guys are afraid for their spots, and they want to stab you in the back. They will give you shit, give you grief just as easily as they'll look at you. D-Von prevented a lot of that by taking me under his wing.

I got away with certain things that I think most rookies don't. Showing up late, cutting in line at the airport. Little things to outsiders, but big things to veterans in the business.

See, veterans like D-Von are afforded certain liberties. He didn't have to show up to the arena early. He could come when he wanted. Which was fine for him, but it wasn't fine for me, not really.

D-Von had all the airline perks that come with being a veteran, not to mention he was a frequent flier. He let me check in with him, so I didn't have to wait in long lines. Truth is, all the rookies had to wait in long lines, and it looked bad for me to go up in front of all the veterans or other guys that had been around longer than I had and breeze through. There are a lot of traditions in this business, and you don't do stuff like that. But I got away with it because I was with D-Von. He made sure I never got slapped for it.

In a lot of places we had main locker rooms and TV locker rooms. There's a pecking order. The older guys who have been around longer use the TV locker rooms, where things aren't as crowded. D-Von would always dress there, and he let me come in. He kind of let me ride his coattails a little bit. Like I say, these things seem like simple things, but in our business, they're not. They're traditions that I was breaking or at least bending, but I was afforded the right to get away with it because I was with D-Von.

Eventually, though, I realized that I had to break away from D-Von and do the right thing on my own. I was almost like a kid who has to leave his parents' house to start earning respect as an adult. I started going to the arenas early, working out, showing my respect for the traditions. D-Von, of course, knew what was going on and let me go ahead on my own. He'd kind of showed me the ropes, then sent me off on my own.

He was always very encouraging. He always said the company had big plans for me. He'd always tell me that. I really respect him and appreciate everything he did for me, giving me what was like a high school education in wrestling. He's a great dude. I love him.

I'M D-VON'S BITCH

Of course, he did bust my chops.

One time, we made this bet. We were in Albuquerque, New Mexico. D-Von was always late to the building and I'd give him shit. D-Von said he was going to come early and work out with me. I was being a smart-ass and said, "If you get to the building early, I'll run around the building naked."

Here's a rule of thumb: never make a bet with a veteran.

I got to the building two hours early . . . but he was already there, waiting.

"Come on," he told me. "Let's go."

I started to take my clothes off. Black Jack Lanza came up and said, "No, no, you can't do that. You're going to get us in trouble if you do that." There were fans outside and everything.

That didn't get me out of my debt, though.

D-Von told me that instead of running around the building naked, I had to give him twenty-five push-ups.

"Pshh. Big fucking deal," I said. "I'll drop down and do 'em with one hand."

He stopped me.

"No, I want them individually," he explained. "And every time after you do a push-up, you have to scream, 'I'm D-Von's bitch!' "

The deal was, I had to do them whenever and wherever he said. No matter what. Even if it was in the middle of a fucking airport.

We'd be out and he'd mutter, "Gimme one."

I'd drop down and shout, "I'm D-Von's bitch!"

Loud, too.

It got to the point where I wouldn't even think twice about it. I actually did all but seven. He let me out of the last seven for some reason that I don't remember now, but I had definitely paid off the debt. To welch would have been unthinkable.

Yeah, I had really good times with D-Von. He was a really good dude.

THE EDGE OF A PIT

I was excited to be up in WWE, but the truth was, I was having a hard time in the ring. I really was not picking it up when I first came in.

Partly, it was because I was always so tense, always trying to remember what I was supposed to do instead of actually doing it. I was always afraid of fucking up. And I still didn't have the skills that I needed for big-time wrestling.

Some people started wondering whether I could make it at all. So did I. The more I screwed up, the more tense I got, and the worse I looked. I had no clue what I was doing and I was lost on the road. My marriage was starting to struggle a little bit because I was always gone. It was extremely rough.

Then, without explanation or warning, they pulled me out of the Reverend D-Von gimmick. They didn't tell us why; they didn't even build a story around it. Which really killed us. One week, I just flipped out on D-Von for really no reason. The next week, I came out on TV and basically killed him, I mean I just beat him in the ring. It was a real short match. I don't know if it was even five minutes long. I came out, and he got on me for a minute or so, then I just nailed him with a Batista bomb. And that was the end of me and D-Von.

They never explained why or what happened; we just went our separate ways. D-Von continued the Reverend gimmick for a short time after that. He reunited with Bubba on *Raw* later on that year.

I wrestled on my own, but I felt like I was in big trouble. My career looked like it was going to wash out. I felt confused, depressed, trapped, embarrassed—you name it. After all those years struggling to climb up a mountain, I stood at the edge of a pit, ready to fall in.

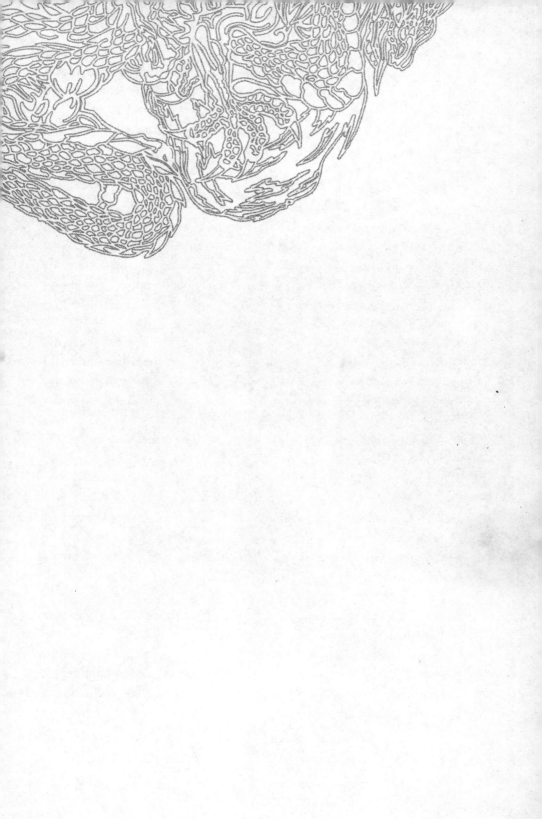

URBANA

Things are a little off at the University of Illinois at Urbana-Champaign Sunday morning when I arrive. There's a problem with the tunnel that leads into the dressing room. When I get there, the local security people want me to park my car in the main lot and then walk around to the locker room. That means I'll have to run a gauntlet of a few hundred fans standing nearby. The ten-minute walk will turn into an hour-long autograph session, and I'll be late for the show. Not to mention give my security people hives.

They finally find an alternate route for me, and one of the local security people volunteers to show it to me. We take a few turns around the campus and pull up in front of what looks like a bunker left over from World War II. There's a door at the side that looks about wide enough for a lawn mower to squeeze through.

"This is it?" I ask as the door opens.

"Yeah," says the security guy. He starts to get out—I think he's under the impression we're walking from here.

But I'm running pretty late.

I hit the gas and squeak the rental car in through the

door. The passage winds underground for what seems like a mile, twisting and turning and not getting any wider as we go. But if you're a wrestler, you're used to squeezing through tight spaces.

Just about when I'm thinking we've taken a wrong turn and gone to Kansas or something, a slit of fluorescent light pokes through the blackness to my left. There's the backstage area, blocked off by a collection of trash canisters. I zip in between them and hop out, tossing the security guy the keys.

"Back it out for me, would you?"

Rumor has it he took early retirement rather than try to squeeze back through the maze.

As the show gets going, it's clear that the audience is a little flat. We can feel it backstage. The fact that the Super Bowl is in a couple of hours may have something to do with it, or maybe it's the heating system, which is fighting a losing battle against the subarctic chill outside. Whatever it is, things just aren't clicking. The wrestlers ahead of me put a lot of extra effort into the show, trying to break through the wall and get the audience inside, but the wall is back and thicker than ever when my match is announced.

Then Ken Kennedy comes out and does this simply great bit. He takes the place over. He starts talking about the Super Bowl and Chicago, pretending at first to be a fan and then, of course, revealing himself as anything but. He'd done something similar the night before, but this afternoon it has real bite. He starts dancing on the Bears—and me—saying we're all going to choke and riling up the crowd.

But that's just for starters.

Someone near the ring yells at him, "You suck!" Kennedy grabs the mike and starts dishing it back.

"I suck, huh? I suck? You're the one that sucks . . ."

I'm sure the audience has heard what he says dozens of times, but somehow he makes it sound original. Within a few seconds, he has the whole arena pissed at him. If there wasn't an army of security between him and the fans, for sure a couple of good ol' boys would come and take him out.

But that's my job. My intro hits and I stalk out. The place isn't just with me—they are riding my back into battle: it is time to put serious hurt into this bastard Mr. Kennedy.

That's what this business is all about. You pray for guys like Kennedy, guys who not only can get the crowd up, but who you can really work with. Guys you can click with. Those are the guys you are going to draw a crowd with. It has to be babyface and heel. Me and Hunter. Me and Eddie. Me and Kennedy. Hunter and Shawn. Stone Cold and The Rock. It's magic.

Victory is not going to be easy today, though. We start out with me pushing him around, but soon he's found my weak knee and he is on it, pounding me relentlessly. I go down. He has his heat—he really has his heat. He's on me, and the fans are on their feet. This is a championship match, and he is wiping my ass all over the ring. I don't think a championship has ever changed hands in a nontelevised event, and these fans know that.

Or at least they did when they came in. Now they're not so damn sure. And in fact, it looks like Kennedy's strategy of stomping my leg is going to win.

"Who sucks now?" he yells, and the place rises to its feet in a rage.

"Batista!" they're yelling. "Batista!"

What they mean is, get the hell up and pound this guy like we know you can. Come on. Come on!!

I use their energy to get up, banged-up leg and all. With the crowd's help, it looks like I might be able to take care of this bastard. But he's got one last trick, tangling my leg with his and pressing until the blood drains from my lower body. I half slip the hold but then I'm over backward, and he's got both of my shoulders down. The ref counts one, two—with every ounce of sweat and strength I break it and the crowd . . . the crowd just explodes.

It is a beautiful thing, a really powerful thing. Because now they're in the ring with us. We're pushing down this bastard Mr. Kennedy, and all the other bastards that have disrespected them in real life. I make the pin and the crowd roars, knowing the victory is as much theirs as it is mine. Their champion has kicked ass, and they've forgotten all about the Super Bowl and the cold and all the other bullshit. They go home happy.

In some ways, a show like today's is more satisfying for a wrestler than one where the crowd is up from the very beginning. You've got to work harder. It's more gratifying when you can start with a crowd that's not very lively, not very loud, not very excited, and by the end of the match, you have them standing on their feet, completely sucked in, their disbelief completely suspended. That's what it's all about.

Certain matches just feel like main events, like big fight matches. This one, even though it was a house show in a chilly arena, had that feel.

Personally, I've never seen a title change on a non-TV match, and I think most if not all the fans at the show today knew that. But we made them believe it could happen. We gave them their money's worth. And even if we had to work a lot harder because they were a rough crowd, that's what it's all about. Man, that's what it's all about.

That's why some days, we don't get much sleep, but we push on anyway. We're tired. It's freezing out here, and the people want to go home and watch the Super Bowl. But we still get the people up on their feet at the end of the match. That feels really good. It's kind of a high, kind of an addiction to this business.

And while the fans are on their way home to go watch the Super Bowl, I grab my things and get on my way to Omaha.

Four

EVOLUTION

D-Von told me once that in terms of my wrestling education, I was in high school when I rode with him, and college when I rode with Triple H and Ric Flair. It's really true. I learned so much from those guys that I can never repay them.

But I might never have graduated from high school to college if David "Fit" Finlay and Chris Benoit hadn't stepped in and helped me get myself straightened out. They were like summer school

Finally, I was able to leave the Deacon behind me.

teachers who you have for a few weeks and then they save your butt just when you're about to wash out. Those teachers never really get any credit, but they may end up changing your life.

PET PROJECT

When my bit with D-Von ended, I was having a lot of trouble in the ring. It wasn't just that I didn't know that much—which was definitely true—I was even having a hard time doing what I knew. I couldn't relax, and that meant I couldn't perform. I had so much to learn and I knew it—and I just couldn't make it work.

I think it was as kind of a last-ditch effort to help me succeed that Johnny Ace said to Fit Finlay, "Batista is your pet project. See if you can do something. Take him under your wing and train him. If he doesn't get better, it's your fault."

That's the story I heard. Whether it's true or not, Finlay really did take me under his wing, and I really did get better.

Finlay has a long history in the business. He started in Ireland and Great Britain, and before coming to WWE he was in the WCW, where he first got attention as "The Belfast Bruiser." He's a guy with tremendous ability and tremendous knowledge about wrestling. Even more important as far as I was concerned, he knows how to communicate it. The guy can teach.

At the time, Dave Taylor had a camp in a suburb of Atlanta called Peach Tree City. Taylor is another veteran originally from England. We went to his camp. There were only four of us: me, Finlay, Taylor, and Chris Benoit.

It's difficult to mention Chris now without thinking of the horrible events in June 2007, when the police say he killed his wife and son and then committed suicide. I don't know what demons were possessing him. The Chris I knew wouldn't have done that.

The week before the murders, he had his wife and son on the road with him. If you saw them, you'd know his son, Daniel, worshiped him, and Chris truly loved his son. And Nancy—well, she always had a smile for everyone.

We were all in Houston for our Pay-Per-View, *Vengeance,* that Sunday, when Chris didn't show up. Everybody was in disbelief—Chris Benoit missing a match? A Pay-Per-View?? So you can just imagine what we felt when we heard the news the next day.

I still can't believe it. It's just so far out of line with what I knew of him.

Up until that tragedy, Chris's career spoke for itself. I loved working with him. He always brought out the best in his opponents. In this case, he came along to help not because we were great friends or anything, but because he thought I was a good guy and worth taking a chance on. He'd do anything to help anybody out, as long as he knew that you wanted to be there.

FINLAY

I should really take a little time here to give a lot of credit to Fit, not just for what he's done for me in my career, but really for what he's done for the business in general. I'm impressed with him on so many different levels it's not even funny. For one, he was out of the ring for I think something like five years, and made probably one of the most successful comebacks that I've ever seen. When everybody heard that he was going to come back into the ring, go from being an agent to a performer, a lot of people smiled behind his back and maybe even laughed a little bit. They were saying things like, "What's he got to contribute?" and "He's past his prime." But now he's a top guy. He's one of the people everyone is begging to work with.

Fit is not the largest guy in stature that you'll ever meet, but he is by far one of the toughest sons of bitches you'll ever meet. A lot of guys in our business are tough, but Fit doesn't feel he has to prove it. He doesn't take liberties on anyone, he doesn't hurt anyone, and isn't too snug. He is naturally snug, though—that first whack from Fit, he really lets you know he's there. But that's the way our business should be. Whenever we're working together and I get that first whack, I say, "You stiff Irish prick." He giggles a little, and we go from there.

Fit is an old-school wrestler. He's one of those guys who, like I've said before, listens to the crowd and works for the moment. He doesn't like to put together big, elaborate spots; he likes to work and create art. Somehow, he never loses sight of the entertainment value and how important that is. He knows wrestling is entertainment. He wants people to believe. He wants it to look like a fight, which it is when you're in there with him, but he's not afraid to make the audience laugh. That's a very delicate balance. And he's not afraid to be the butt of the joke. That's something Eddie Guerrero had, too. He wants to make the match look like a shoot, like it's real, but he also wants to entertain you.

Like his leprechaun, who really has added a lot to our shows, just fun stuff. I'm pretty sure Hornswoggle was his idea. It's kind of crazy when you think about it—especially considering Fit and what a tough son of a bitch he is—having a leprechaun hiding under the ring to be part of his act, but that's who he is.

Now, Fit might not like me to say this, but outside the ring he's a very compassionate person. He's not afraid to be kind. It's impressive today in general, but it's especially impressive in our business. He's a true gentleman.

One last thing: I've always noticed and admired how proud he is of his family and his kids. A couple of times he's brought his kids over, you see him gleaming, just glowing, because he's so proud of those kids. That's awesome. That's a dad.

STRETCHED INTO THE MOMENT

These guys had the same kind of working styles and philosophies on wrestling. They're all very, very talented men. They really stretched the shit out of me from the very first minute I got there.

I mean that literally. They'd put me in a hold and kind of stretch me a little bit, not to hurt me, just to work me out. They took turns. One guy would get in the ring and wrestle a little bit, doing a lot of mat wrestling, a little chain wrestling. When he was blown up, a fresh guy came in to take his place. Meanwhile I'm still blown, I'm tired and struggling. But they were in there pushing me, seeing how bad I wanted it. They ran me into the ground. I lost ten pounds of water weight every day I was there.

I ended up getting a lot of heat later on because I said that I learned more from Finlay in two days or whatever than I learned from OVW in two years. Jim Cornette never forgave me for saying that. But it was true. I never really learned how to work at OVW. I learned how to kill guys in squash matches, Goldberg-type matches. You go in and just obliterate the guy, like Bill Goldberg did in his undefeated run at the start of his WCW career.

Well, down in Atlanta, they picked up on it right away. As soon as they put me in a move, I would try to get out of it. The guys told me to live in the moment. Don't get ahead of yourself. Somebody's got you in a hold, you work to get out of that hold, you don't just pop out of it.

Live in the moment.

For me, that was the main difference between what I had been doing and what I should have been doing. That was the key to making it all believable. It changed everything. I realized that wrestling wasn't about going through the motions and knowing all the moves. It's about working, taking your time in the ring, and getting it right.

Things didn't start turning around right away. It wasn't like in a movie or a television show, where your whole life changes in one sixty-second scene. But it definitely turned on a lightbulb in my head. It gave me a new outlook on wrestling. I realized it was an art, not a science.

WRESTLING IS AN ART

There are a handful of guys who are so good, they can go out and call a match on the fly with literally anyone and still have a five-star match any day of the week. Guys like Ric Flair, guys like Triple H, guys like Stone Cold, The Rock. Those guys. They are naturals, and they are the best. There's only a handful of them, and however they got there, through whatever combination of hard work and natural ability, they're in a special class by themselves. They make it happen, and it seems, at least to me, that they never struggle doing it.

But for me, wrestling is an art that takes patience and practice and, above all, work. There's much more to wrestling than just knowing the moves. In a way, it's the art of selling. You have to get in the moment and feed off the crowd and make it real. You sell not the moves, but what's behind the moves. Everybody knows it's entertainment, and that makes it harder, because you're trying to suck them in. But if you really live in the moment, make the people believe, they will. Because they want to believe.

EVOLUTION

When I got back to WWE, they had me start working with Triple H and Randy Orton. They were getting me ready for Evolution.

Evolution was a heel group that was modeled after the Four Horsemen. People who are familiar with wrestling history know that the original Four Horsemen—Ric Flair, Arn Anderson, Ole Anderson, and Tully Blanchard—were extremely popular heels in the late 1980s. Though traditionally heels are bad guys who fans boo, the Four Horsemen had a tremendous following and great success in the ring. They had swagger and flash, and really lived it up with the women. The group went through a couple of different incarnations over the years, but the basic premise never really changed.

Evolution was a heel stable for the new century, but otherwise we were modeled exactly on the Four Horsemen. Everything from the way we dressed, to the way we carried ourselves, to what we bragged about was based on that.

Evolution was so cool, it was hard to hate us, even though we were big-time heels. We were four badasses. We had a style and a profile. We were getting all the girls. We were having fun. Running things. Beating up whoever got in our way. In the wrestling world, how could you not love that?

I believe Evolution was Hunter's idea. He wanted to do it, and he picked me and Randy. He thought he could turn us into stars and give us big futures in the company. And he did. Hunter created two world champions.

HUNTER

Hunter, of course, is Hunter Hearst-Helmsley, aka Paul Michael Levesque, and known probably to every wrestling fan in the world as Triple H. I don't know that there has ever been a better, more natural, more successful heel in professional wrestling. As I mentioned earlier, Hunter is one of the very few wrestlers who is in a class by himself.

Fans have recognized his talent from his early days in WCW, though I guess you could say that he didn't really come into his own until he left for World Wrestling Federation in 1995. I've heard it said that he's held more world championships than anyone in WWE's history.

I believe he'd been thinking about the Evolution concept and including me in it for a long time. I had heard rumors about the group—or "stable," as some call it—ever since I came up to WWE, though when they stuck me in the goofy suit, I thought there was no way it was going to happen. Putting me in that suit, though, had been smart. Because I couldn't just use my body—I couldn't just be big and intimidating—I had learned to act a little. Even though it confused the hell out of me, it helped me grow.

"FUCKING RELAX"

Hunter is a tremendous store of wrestling technique and know-how, but probably the most valuable thing he taught me had to do with attitude.

His advice:

"Fucking relax."

Just like that. "Fucking relax." I can still hear his voice telling me that. "Fucking relax. Why you so wound up? Everyone fucks up. I fuck up. That's where you learn. That's what you do when you fuck up, it makes you, you know, it makes you."

Him saying that put me at ease in the ring. I started having more fun and paying attention to the crowd.

Technique-wise, there were countless suggestions he made that improved my act. Simple suggestions that ended up making a big difference.

I used to set up my finish by using a spinebuster. I'd use a spinebuster and then go directly to the finish.

Now, I hope everyone reading this knows what a spinebuster is, but just in case: the move starts with me facing my opponent. I grab him around the waist, elevate him, then slam him to the mat. There are a couple of different variations to the basic spinebuster; when you put a spin in there you're paying homage to Arn Anderson, who made that variation so famous a lot of people call it the Anderson Spinebuster.

My spinebuster would daze my opponent and lead directly to my finish—and again, I really hope you know this—the Batista bomb. When I first started, it was really a quick progression: spinebuster, bomb—one-two-three and out.

"Man, I wish you had something there to call for your finish," Hunter told me. "To let people know you were going for the finish."

He wanted me to watch a tape, I think it was from *WrestleMania*, of a big match between Hogan and Ultimate Warrior. He felt Hogan had a way of making matches have a big-fight feeling. So when we watched it together, I saw Ultimate Warrior and his intensity. Hunter suggested I shake the ropes before I go for my big finish. That's where all that comes from.

It's a simple suggestion, but it makes a big difference. When I shake the ropes, the crowd knows I'm coming for my big finish. They lose their minds. They're into it and the finish is that much better.

THE BATISTA BOMB

Shane McMahon actually recommended that I do the Batista bomb as my finish. This was soon after I first came up. He thought it would be cool, because he never really saw any big guys doing it. Of course, it wasn't called the Batista bomb then. I think it was J.R.—Jim Ross—who dubbed it the Batista bomb. It's really just a sit-out powerbomb. There are a bunch of other names for the move, Tiger bomb is one. It looks fairly simple, but you need a bit of strength to pull it off.

For maybe the one person reading this who hasn't seen it: the move is generally set up by action that's left your opponent dazed and confused, in my case, the spinebuster. You grab him and stick his head between your legs. Then you curl your arms around his waist, and lift and spin him up so that he ends up sitting on your shoulders. At that point, your opponent is basically toast, because your next move is to bring him to the canvas really fast by sitting down.

The slam knocks what little sense he has left out of him. Most of my opponents are so wiped that all I have to do is lean on them to get the pin. It's such a big move and makes such a huge noise that it looks and feels like a finish. Nobody's going to get up from it. It even leaves me a little dazed.

It didn't take long to learn. I can't remember who I practiced it with, but we went down one day and did it on a crash mat. I think I began using it the same night. It was one of those things where the crowd liked it right away. It's pretty devastating. Like I said, it's a big move and it makes such a huge noise: it looks and feels like a finish. Nobody's going to get up from it.

It does take a bit of strength to pull off. It's also one of those moves that takes two. A lot of times, especially if it's a bigger guy, if they don't crunch up for me it's just impossible. Even when they do, it can be hard. There was one match I did where I was actually working with Kane, and I was really sick. He's bigger than I am and between being sick and

Laying the Batista bomb on Gregory Helms, Hurricane.

mis-timing the move, I couldn't get him all the way up. I think I got him halfway up and he dropped back down.

That was a match that didn't go well, obviously. People shit all over it. They started booing. Then there was another where I did the same thing with Booker. I got him halfway up and had to bring him down, because we had mistimed it or something. But I actually snatched him and went back up with it and never let him go. That one I salvaged.

Usually, though, it's up, down, count him out.

ANIMAL

I mentioned The Warlord earlier, and his connection with the Road Warriors and the original Animal, Joseph Laurinaitis. He's a real big guy who grew up in poor neighborhoods and worked as a bouncer before he got into pro wrestling. Some people might think there was a connection there between us, but the truth is that my nickname as Animal was something that just evolved on its own. I didn't even have anything to do with it.

I believe Jim Ross dubbed me the Animal. He started saying that I wrestled like an animal or that I had an animalistic style to my wrestling, something like that. I think he meant that I was more a brawler than a technical wrestler. And I was a big guy, so I had that beast image, hovering over guys and being relentless and ruthless. Nothing pretty about it.

The name came about during Evolution, though I don't quite remember when. It fit, though, and it stuck—one of J.R.'s many inventions over his long and illustrious career.

HEELS

As a heel with Evolution, I started getting booed. A lot.

I took pride in that. It meant I was doing my job.

I think being a heel is a lot of fun. You know, you can't have a kick-ass babyface unless you have a kick-ass heel. It's like good and evil: no evil, no good. It just goes hand in hand.

There have been some great heels in pro wrestling. I've always preferred cool heels to, say, a chickenshit heel. Hunter's cool; he has that rebel thing going that you can't take away from him under any circumstance. When he's a heel, he's a badass, an ass-kicking heel. Those are the kinds of heels I like.

Ric Flair and Hunter of course come to mind when you mention cool heels, but there have been a lot of others. To me, Stone Cold Steve Austin was always a heel. People loved him so much, but he was a heel. He was just a badass, ass-kicking, rednecked heel. Because he was *so* over with the crowd, people turned him into a babyface. But to me, he'll always be a cool heel.

Then there's Arn Anderson.

ARN ANDERSON

Arn—his real name is Martin Lunde—had such a great career in wrestling that I can hardly sum it up in a few words. He's worked with the biggest names in the industry: Ric, Ole Anderson, Dusty Rhodes, Sgt. Slaughter—it just goes on and on. Right now Arn works as a producer or road agent for WWE. Road agents help wrestlers develop story lines, work on moves, and in general help us do what we have to do in the ring.

I tried to model myself after Arn, because Arn was the enforcer in the Four Horsemen, and I was the enforcer in Evolution. So I really tried to get with him every chance I could, just to pick his brain and be a sponge around him. I learned so much from him it's ridiculous. I'm often guilty of not giving him credit. And most of what I learned were little things, the simple subtleties of being a heel.

Arn has always been real big on making things very simple. As a wrestler, he would do things people could relate to. They weren't huge spots. Like he'd kick somebody in the knee. You kick somebody in the knee, that's dirty. That hurts. It's something nasty, especially if you're a guy like me who's big and usually wrestles guys who are smaller.

Why would somebody my size kick somebody in the knee? Why? Because I'm a dirty fucking prick. I'm a nasty-ass heel.

Arn taught me something else that has always stuck with me. Heels make you uncomfortable. One example: when I was in the ring beating up on somebody, he suggested I lean in over them. He told me to get uncomfortably close. Hover over them, be in their space. It's a bully thing.

That's what a heel is.

Arn was never a big physical specimen. But he made people hate him. He was just a nasty prick in the ring. I wish Arn had extended his career, because I would have loved to have had a chance to work with him in the ring. He was forced to retire because of injuries. Wrestling fans missed out on a lot when he went out.

ARN AND RIC

The funny thing is that even though Arn and Ric are the greatest of friends, really big friends, Arn would just cringe at some of the things that Ric does in the ring. Arn is very serious, a brutal, serious heel. Ric is just— well, over the top.

Hilariously goofy.

Ric is famous for doing a spot where a guy will give him a sunset flip and end up pulling his trunks down. Ric will run around the ring with his ass hanging out while the crowd roars.

We were doing six-man tags with me, Hunter, and Ric during Evolution. They wanted to do a three-way thing where we would do a triple sunset flip and end up with our trunks down, running around the ring. I at first refused to do it. My character was serious; I had the enforcer role and it didn't seem to fit. But Ric and Hunter did it, and of course everybody loved it. So Ric and Hunter gave me shit about it, just tons of heat, so the next night we all did it. Of course, we made total asses of ourselves—excuse the pun—running around with our trunks down to our knees, dragging guys around behind us.

Arn Anderson was the agent on the house show, and he was backstage. We walked back into the locker room and there he was, up on a chair, one end of his belt tied around his neck, the other in his hand about to be tied to a pipe.

He'd seen enough. He was about ready to hang himself.

It was one of the funniest things I've ever seen.

BOUNCING FOR THE FACES

Part of being a successful heel is making people hate you. You watch someone like Mr. Kennedy, for example. He just goes out and practically from the first word out of his mouth he's egging on the crowd. He just riles them up until any one of them would give a year's salary to spit in his face.

But there's a lot more to being a successful heel than getting people to hate you. When we were in Evolution, we were badass heels, but look what we did for the guys who came in against us. We'd bounce around for them and make them look like a million fuckin' dollars.

Even guys who weren't the best workers, in terms of making a match look real. Take Goldberg, for instance. He's a great guy, but he'll tell you, he's not the best worker. He has a hard time with the psychology and story that you tell inside the ring; it's hard for him to translate that into something with his body that sucks the fans in. The people he works with have to do a good job to make the match look good.

A babyface's success depends a great deal on the heels he's facing. It's all in how you make them look. A good heel will make your babyface look like Superman. Or you get a guy like Scottie Steiner, who was an awesome worker, but by the time he came to the company, he physically was having so many problems that it was hard for him to do anything. And he's a great guy, by the way, so I don't by any means want to show him any disrespect. Take nothing away from Scottie. His matches when he was at his peak were excellent, entertaining as hell. But by the time he got to our company, he had a lot of physical problems. He really needed a break. We'd bounce around for him and by the time we were done he looked like the baddest motherfucker on the planet. Even with Randy Orton—who started out as a heel with us on Evolution—when we turned Randy into a babyface and started bouncing around for Randy, by the time we were done, Randy was the *man*.

Doesn't happen without a good heel.

SUSPENDING DISBELIEF

There's a technical term that we use in our business for sucking the audience into the show. We say we're trying to get the audience to "suspend its disbelief." I think the phrase actually comes from theater, but it really fits pro wrestling.

The first time I heard it was when I was at OVW. Jim Ross came down and talked to us. He was still head of talent relations back then and he gave us a whole lecture on it. I didn't know what the fuck he meant at first. Even when I understood the words, it took a long time to translate them into things that I could do.

People come into a wrestling event or turn on the television knowing that what we do is entertainment. They don't believe it's real. In order for us to entertain them, we have to get them past that disbelief. Basically, we're making them forget that they're watching entertainment. We don't want people to say, "Gee, that looked fake." We want people to say, "God, that looks like it fucking hurt."

Sometimes the way we do that is by doing things that do really hurt.

I'll give you an example. Probably my favorite match of all time was a Hell in a Cell match with Triple H at the *Vengeance* Pay-Per-View not too long after I'd won the championship for the first time. We used a chair wrapped in barbed wire for the show.

The cameras did a close-up after he whacked me and you could see the blood spurting out of the holes in my back.

This isn't the sort of thing kids should be copying, by the way. The stunt was carefully thought out and planned.

We didn't do any rehearsals, though—I only wanted to go through that once. It's one of those things where you just kind of brace yourself and say, "Fucking hit me!"

And he did.

But whether it's big spots or little spots, these things are tools we use to get people sucked into the match. Once we get them on the edge of their seats and make them want to see who's going to win, that's when they're in the palms of our hands. That's the art of it. And that's not easy to do.

MR. MAGOO

Right at the start of Evolution, I rode in a car with Ric, Hunter, and Randy Orton. The old-timers will tell you, you learn more in the car than you learn anywhere else. Believe it. If you get with a veteran, you're going to get schooled. You leave a show and the match is still fresh in your mind. The older guys will tell you what you did wrong, and what you should try. Do this, do that. They take it apart for you. They also tell stories about how what you did relates to something somebody did five, ten, twenty years ago. There's this great oral tradition that goes back, way back. Riding with Ric and Hunter was like getting an advanced seminar in wrestling every night.

But being in the car with them was fun, too. They were entertaining as hell, whether they were telling stories or just doing funny stuff.

I have to say Ric and Hunter are two of the messiest guys I've ever known. They would start the day off with a nice clean shirt. By the end of the day, *both* of them would have stuff all over their shirts. Ric would start it off in the morning, because he never got in the car without a cup of coffee. It never failed; there'd be coffee all over his shirt within minutes. If we went out to eat, both of them would get barbecue sauce and whatever splattered all over themselves. They'd dip their cuffs in their drinks. They were just messy.

Driving itself was an adventure. Hunter used to always refer to Ric as Mr. Magoo. I think Ric's legally blind in one eye. And he's very easily distracted. His wife, Tiffany, always says that he's got adult ADD—attention-deficit disorder—and that he'll stop at everything that distracts him. He'll go, "Ooh, something shiny!" That's it, he's distracted. He starts talking, he gets distracted.

Put those two things together when you're driving, and you're going to get lost. A lot. And Ric is always lost.

But he insisted on driving. One time, we were going to Norfolk to do a show. Ric was at the wheel and we were lost, of course. We were completely on the wrong side of town. Ric tried to convince me and Hunter that they had moved the highway from one side of Norfolk to the other, and that's why we were lost, not because he had taken the wrong turn or anything.

"I'm telling you, I've been coming here for thirty years," he said. "They moved the freaking highway."

He was *serious*. And Hunter started giving him shit, and Ric started getting hot, trying to convince us they moved the highway from one side of the city to the other side of the city. He just insisted he was right.

It wasn't uncommon for Ric to go up a one-way street the wrong way, or to go ninety miles in the wrong direction. But we were always so entertained by him that we didn't learn our lesson and kept letting him drive.

LIFE LESSONS

To this day, I won't take driving directions from Ric, but I always tell people that Ric has taught me tons in the ring, and more about life.

Ric is one of those guys who enjoys every second he's breathing. He makes life tolerable on the road. He finds the best in every place he goes. He's one of those guys who seems to bring the party around with him. He has a good time, enjoys life, and shares that joy. If he's there, the party's there. He just enjoys people.

I can't really pinpoint a specific wrestling lesson he taught me. Ric

Typically, Ric makes Hunter and me look like we don't know what we are doing.

never sat down and said, "Here, let me teach you this move." It was really more about wrestling as an art form. How to get the crowd on their feet. How to get the most out of your match. When and where to do things, where to put things in your match, at what point you want to start bringing the crowd up. I learned by watching him do it.

Sometimes it took a while to figure it out. We used to do six-man tag matches a lot in Evolution. Sometimes Ric would lose us.

Hunter and I would be standing in the corner and Ric would be in the ring. We'd look at each other, baffled.

"What the hell's he doing?" Hunter would ask.

I wouldn't have a clue. He was out there improvising on his own, and he was four or five steps ahead of us. He'd go through all these things and we'd finally realize he was making up something that moment to suck the crowd in.

That was really the thing that made him so good: he knew how to read a crowd.

I think a lot of fans don't really know why certain matches are better than others. I don't think they can pinpoint it. But I think subconsciously, they know one guy's match is a lot better than another guy's match.

For the most part, we all do the same moves, so there may not *seem* to be that much of a difference. But the way Ric explained it, a lot of the difference comes from when and where you put those moves in. It's how you sell the feeling to the crowd. A move at the right time has much more impact than the same move, or even a better one, at the wrong time.

For Ric, it comes down to listening to the crowd. If you're paying attention to the crowd, waiting for them, pumping them up and giving them what they want—then you have a great match. Two different sets of guys can have two identical matches, doing the same moves in the same order. One set listens to the audience, takes its cue from the fans, really sells the match. The other set doesn't. Who's going to have the crowd on their feet by the end of the day?

I think you can learn that—I did—but I also think that certain guys have more of an instinct for it than others. I think Randy Orton, for example, has it naturally. Maybe because he grew up in the business. He had more instincts for it.

RANDY ORTON

Randy didn't last too long riding around with us. I think he felt like he was riding around with a bunch of old guys. He needed to be with guys who were a few years younger, a little more tuned to a younger lifestyle, younger tastes. He can be such a moody bastard, too. You couldn't be moody in front of Ric or Hunter.

Randy came at the business from a much different angle than I did. His father is Cowboy Bob Orton, who's in the WWE Hall of Fame. His grandfather was The Big O—Bob Orton, Sr.—and his uncle was Barry Orton. Their friends included guys like Andre the Giant and Roddy Piper. Weekend gatherings at the Orton house were like wrestling hall of fame shows.

Like me, Randy put in his time at OVW, coming over to WWE in 2002. He's got a great look and great physical strength. Even though he's run into some troubles during his career, I still think he's got intense potential.

My thumbs-up, thumbs-down thing came out of something involving Randy when Hunter kicked him out of Evolution. Of course, it was kind of a ripoff from the Roman Empire and the gladiators in the Colosseum. Thumbs-up, thumbs-down, does the gladiator live or die?

Then later on I did it to Hunter when I turned on him. Vince McMahon saw it and loved it so much that he wanted me to keep doing it. Now people get with it. They throw their thumbs up with me, then down with me. They're ready for the finish. They're calling for me to feed my opponent to the lions. And I'm happy to oblige.

STONE COLD

I was lucky enough to get to work with Stone Cold a little bit during Evolution. Physically, he was still recovering from his neck injury, so it was a pretty small spot. But it was still a thrill for me.

I went out and had a little physicality with him in the ring. I can't remember what it was, but he wanted me to start beating him up. And it was one of those things where I'm saying to myself, "This is Stone Cold Steve Austin. I don't want to mess up."

I forget exactly what I did, but at one point I suggested he do something to me. He said, "No, go ahead. This is for you, kid. Get yourself over."

He let me beat up on him a bit. He was very generous about it. He was trying to give me a little rub, and he did.

There was another time we were doing a backstage television vignette together. He was very helpful. I remember him saying, "Why don't you do it like this?" And he got up in my face and he started doing my lines.

"Does that feel uncomfortable to you?" he asked when he was done.

I said, "Yeah, it really does."

"That's how it should feel."

Exactly. When you get a lesson like that from Stone Cold Steve Austin, you don't forget it.

I don't know Steve that well. But I do know that when Stone Cold walks through that fucking curtain, there aren't many people in the world who can compare to him. He's a phenomenon.

His Austin 3:16 (". . . I just whipped your ass!") and his Stone Cold single-finger salute were where that whole WWE attitude thing came from. He's got an electricity about him. He would make the whole crowd stand up on their feet just with his entrance alone.

But he's another one of those guys who is no great physical specimen. He's not huge by any means. You'll never look at him out on the street and think, This guy could kill me with his bare hands if he wanted to. When he hits the ring, though, he's the baddest motherfucker on the planet. He's got the it factor coming out of his ass. When he's in character, he believes it, and the crowd believes it. He also happens to be one of the best workers of all time.

The funny thing is, he got fired from WCW before he came over to our company. I believe Eric Bischoff, who was running WCW at the time, said he wasn't going to amount to shit. And look what he did. He really changed the whole tone of wrestling. He's a good dude. I wish I knew him a little better, because I'd sit down and pick his brain.

Man, I bet he has some fucking stories.

STEAL THE SHOW

Not all of the advice I received in my early days in Evolution came from other wrestlers. Some of the best advice came from the boss.

Soon after I started in Evolution, Vince McMahon pulled me aside. I was still tentative. I wasn't wrestling very aggressively, and Vince knew it. He felt that I should be more full of piss and vinegar.

"What the fuck's wrong with you? Why don't you have a little attitude?" he told me. "You walk around here, you always try to stay low-key. It's good to be humble, but we really need you to have a little bit of an attitude."

This is the boss of the company telling me this. Forget his character on the show—this is the guy who made sport entertainment what it is today.

"Dave, I want you to get in there and be aggressive. I want you to steal the show," he said. "I'm giving you license to do whatever the fuck you want."

He wanted me to be a star. He wanted me to steal the spotlight. He encourages that. Vince loves hams—guys who are going out there trying to steal the spotlight. That's where it gets competitive. We're trying to top each other. That's all part of being a star in this business.

It's not easy to steal the spotlight with guys like Ric and Hunter right next to you. But that's what I had to do if I wanted to succeed, and Vince made that clear.

VINNY MAC

Vince is a fucking character. I think a lot of people take him wrong. Don't get me wrong, he can be a fucking asshole. He's ripped me apart on a few occasions. But I think deep down, Vince is just a real locker-room guy, one of the boys. He's down to earth. Probably even a little bit shy. He's someone you can always talk to on any level; you don't have to talk business with him. He's even interested in goofy shit that happens on the road. "Hey, Vince, I was out last night, and this hot girl showed me her tits." He loves to hear those stories.

But Vinny Mac is the *boss*.

Right before the last *Survivor Series* in 2006, when I won the title back, I blew off a photo shoot I was supposed to do. I had a reason for blowing it off. I had been scheduled for appearances on both of the days just before it, one in New York on Friday, one in Houston on Saturday. That Saturday night I had to fly up to Philadelphia. By the time I got back to Philly, it was late and I was exhausted. The next day was going to be a big deal for me, because I was going to win the title back in the *Survivor Series*. So I decided to get some sleep and not go to the photo shoot that Sunday morning. I didn't think it was a big deal.

I got a call from Vince. He started ripping me apart, saying I was being unprofessional. Which I thought was kind of ridiculous. I mean, I *was* busting my ass here, but then I missed one thing and rather than being tired or something, bam, I'm unprofessional.

I started laughing, kind of out of a little bit out of nerves, I guess. The more I laughed, the more pissed he got. He really laid into me. Vince is one of those guys, he's pretty intimidating. By the end of that phone call, I felt about two inches tall.

I haven't missed a photo shoot since, and don't plan to, either. Tired or not.

Vince also trains harder than most of the guys I've ever met in my life. Which always impresses the piss out of me. I watched Vince go through a couple of training sessions. He used to train with this guy Gary who was in security for us for a while. Man, they literally busted their asses. You think a guy sixty years old is not going to train that hard, but man, he's hard-core.

THE COURSE OF EVOLUTION

The Evolution story line built up from late fall 2002 until the end of January 2003, when the "stable" was officially announced. Ric and Hunter were the heart of Evolution; they linked the past and present together. Randy and I were seen by a lot of people as the future. Some of our best opponents over the year and a half or so that Evolution ran included Kane, Scott Steiner, Booker T, Shawn Michaels, Chris Benoit, Edge, Chris

Jericho, Goldberg, Shelton Benjamin, and Maven. I've probably forgotten a few; blame it on the bumps they gave me in the ring.

In his book, *To Be the Man*, Ric talks a little bit about how great an honor it was for him to be part of Evolution. He also talks about Hunter and how great a performer he was. According to Ric, Hunter had been talking about putting Evolution together from the beginning of 2002. Ric talks about how Evolution seemed to complete a circle in his career. For me, it was an incredible launch.

At one point—*Armageddon 2003*—we held all of the WWE championships: the World Tag Team Championship (Ric and I), the WWE Intercontinental Championship (Randy), and the World Heavyweight Championship (Triple H). But before that happened, both Randy and I went out with injuries.

TRICEPS

We'd only been doing Evolution for a few months when I tore my triceps in March 2003. I felt terrible at the time, because I was working my way toward my first *WrestleMania*, at that point only about a month away. The injury was pretty serious and took me out of play for several months.

Randy got injured in the same match. It was brutal. We were in Pennsylvania, doing the television show. It was freezing cold, and we didn't get a chance to warm up or anything before we went on. Randy and I were facing the Dudley Boys—Bubba Ray Dudley and D-Von Dudley—in a tag team match.

Right off the bat, I ran into Bubba awkwardly. I felt my triceps strain. The triceps is the long muscle that runs along the underside and back of your arm. Most of the time, we take it for granted, but if it weren't there, we'd never be able to extend our forearm or have our shoulder muscles do any useful work.

My arm felt funny, but it didn't really hurt; it didn't feel as if I'd completely torn anything, though I could tell I'd done something a little more extreme than a pull. So anyway, I started wrestling in the match and my arm started hurting a little more. Then a little more, then a lot more.

I went over and tagged Randy, and told him I did something to my arm.

I swear not more than thirty seconds later, he came back and was tagging me, saying, "I think I broke my foot."

I'm laughing just thinking about this, but it wasn't very funny then.

"Well, my arm's killing me," I told him.

I went in just the same. D-Von was in the ring with me, and I told him I did something to my arm. He called a spot while I had him in a hold and I reminded him, "Hey, I got something wrong with my arm."

I forget now exactly what he wanted me to do, but I think he wanted me to catch him in a cross-body block. In a cross-body, which is also sometimes called a flying cross-body, one wrestler jumps onto you, ordinarily across your chest, and puts you down to the mat. Two good hands to catch the other guy are pretty much required, which is why I wanted him to do something else.

For some reason D-Von ran the spot anyway. I caught him, but as soon as I hit the mat, I felt this hot, excruciating pain. My triceps had been ripped.

BUBBA DUDLEY IS AN ASSHOLE

The match continued for a while, and it was just a nightmare. When it ended, they hauled Randy out in an ambulance. I followed in a car. Even Bubba Dudley got hurt, injuring his back.

Or so he claimed.

See, the thing that really, really drives me crazy about that night was that Bubba Dudley bitched out Randy while he was being put into the ambulance. Bubba started yelling at Randy, claiming that because of landing on Randy's foot, he had hurt his back.

Excuse me?

Because Bubba *broke* Randy's foot by landing on it and *crushing* it, Bubba's back *hurt* and it was *Randy's fault.*

Yeah, that's it. Randy's in the ambulance with a broken foot and Bubba's screaming and yelling at him.

And you know, usually if somebody gets injured in your match, or even if it's just a guy you work with, at some point you try to give him a call to check on him and see how he's doing. You want to show a little bit of concern. He's a coworker, and whether you were responsible or not, it's just a polite thing to do. The *right* thing to do. Show you care.

Needless to say, Bubba never gave me or Randy a call just to see how we were doing. Nothing.

In my opinion, Bubba Dudley is a jerk-off. He's one of those people who used to always bully guys and throw his weight around just because he had a good position in the company. He'd been around for a long time and he was one of those veterans who'd always treated the rookies like shit. He treated me like shit. He treated Randy like shit. To this day, I can't forgive him.

I don't have a whole lot of bad things to say about people, but Bubba Dudley will always be a piece of shit in my book.

MY FIRST BAD INJURY

So anyway, I went to the hospital and had an MRI done. It told me my triceps was torn. I had to have surgery to repair the tear. Of course, injuries are an occupational hazard for wrestlers, but this was the first really bad injury I'd had. It took me out of the ring for nearly seven months.

Part of the reason I was out so long was that I reinjured myself maybe two and a half months after the surgery. I was trying to get back into shape. I was gung ho, and was looking forward to starting to work out and get back into full shape so I could wrestle again. But while I was out running, I fell and re-tore the muscle. I just fell and landed on it wrong and it popped apart again. It actually didn't hurt that much, but it was obvious that I'd torn it. I guess I hadn't had enough time to heal and the repair wasn't strong enough yet.

For some reason, people started spreading stories about what happened. I just don't know why they'd do that, but they did. People were spreading rumors on the Internet that I was on a treadmill and fell off and re-tore it. Others "suspected" I was in the gym lifting weights and I re-tore it. It's kind of strange that people spend energy coming up with stories about things that they have no idea about.

Not to discount the physical injury, but I believe I hurt emotionally more than anything else. It was pretty heartbreaking. I'd been really hoping to be in *WrestleMania* that year, and of course that couldn't happen. And, since I was still new with Evolution, I was afraid that I would lose my spot. No matter what anybody tells you, I think you're always just a little bit afraid that if something goes wrong it will blow your career. At least that's the way I felt.

And they did start talking about replacing me. If I'm not mistaken, at one point they even looked at guys who might take my slot. I was very fortunate that Hunter felt strongly that Evolution wouldn't be the same without me. So they held out and waited through the spring and summer for me. That's a very long time in the wrestling world. I'm still thankful for that.

I should also probably mention that most wrestlers don't get paid while they're injured. In my case, I went back to my guaranteed salary, which wasn't that much; it was barely enough for me to live on, though I was grateful for any income at that point.

Of course, when I came back to work, because I had already exceeded my guarantee, in effect I had to pay the money back. Which really sucked.

Wrestlers are paid according to a complicated formula. When you get hurt, you don't get paid anywhere near your normal salary.

So you might think about that the next time you hear or read a rumor about someone faking an injury.

I'M BACK

I remember my first night back was on *Raw*, October 20, 2003. We were in Wilkes-Barre, Pennsylvania. I did a run-in on Goldberg, flattening him. According to the story, Hunter had put a contract out on Goldberg, and I saw that as the perfect opportunity to get myself back into the ring.

Coming back against Goldberg was big for me on a personal level, because Bill was one of the guys I really followed when I started watching pro wrestling again as an adult, just before I made the decision to try it myself. I was a huge Goldberg fan. I still am, as a matter of fact.

Bill made his name in wrestling with an undefeated string in WCW in the late 1990s. He won something like 173 matches—some sources give different numbers—from the very beginning of his career until a match against Kevin Nash in 1998 at WCW's *Starcade* Pay-Per-View, a fight he lost because Nash's friend Scott Hall nailed him with a taser. His streak included a win over Hulk Hogan for the WCW championship in July 1998. After WCW was bought by World Wrestling Federation, he wrestled for a short time in Japan and then in 2003 came over to WWE; he wrestled with the company for about a year before retiring.

The thing that made Goldberg and especially his unbeaten string so impressive was his intensity. You just believed he was wiping the mat with these guys. God knows he's not the best worker in the world—Bill admits it himself. But that intensity. He just makes people believe. And he's a great guy in real life. I can't think of one bad thing to say about him. I don't think anyone could.

A STIFF PRICK

That match in 2003 was the first time I'd ever faced Goldberg in the ring. It was brief—I did my run-in, grabbed a chair, and crushed his ankle. It was supposed to put him out of business for good.

Of course, the next week he came back with a cast on and killed us all. He beat the shit out of Evolution for the next few months.

I mean that literally. Goldberg is one stiff prick.

I'm joking, because he's such a great guy with a big heart and a good sense of humor. Bill really is "stiff" in wrestling terms. For anyone who's still new to the sport, stiff means that the wrestler hits his opponents harder than most other wrestlers do, not because he's trying to hurt them, but because he can't make the spot or whatever look real without doing that.

Bill would never intentionally hurt anybody. He's just a big, strong, physical guy, and a lot of his stuff looked real because it *was* real. We'd bounce around for him in the ring and by the end of the match we'd be lying on the mat, bruised and battered.

I'd yell over at Randy, "Randy, you okay?"

"Yeah, I'm okay. Hunter, you okay?"

"Yeah, I'm okay. Batista?"

"I'm still here, man."

We always checked with each other to make sure we got out alive.

BUSTED NOSE

Sometimes the most dangerous time for a wrestler isn't during a match. What's that statistic or saying about bathtubs being the most dangerous places in the world? Whatever it is, I can top it—a birthday cake busted my nose.

We were in Seattle doing *Raw*—this must have been toward the tail end of 2004, though I've forgotten exactly when. Anyway, we did this thing where we had a huge cake set up in the ring. It was supposed to be a celebration of Evolution's birthday, because we'd been together for a year or so. A stripper was supposed to come out the top. I'm sure you've seen the gag a million times.

Except this time, instead of a stripper, Randy Orton popped out. He jumps out and the first shot he throws is an elbow to my nose.

Bam. He shattered it. My nose exploded all over the place. It was still bleeding later that night on the red-eye flight back east.

I couldn't get it fixed for something like two months, because I couldn't take time off until our Christmas break. It swelled up to about twice its normal size. Not only was it broken, but my septum was deviated. The septum is the cartilage in the nose that separates your nostrils into two separate paths for you to breathe through. Screw it up badly enough and you have trouble breathing. In my case, there were days it was almost impossible to breathe, and my asthma didn't help much. A lot of nights I couldn't sleep. I was one miserable son of a bitch until I finally got it fixed.

I think the week or so after surgery was even worse. I had these tubes shoved up my nose to keep the passages open and I was so irritable and grouchy that my wife went and stayed with her mother. She just had to get away because I was being such an ass. I couldn't blame her, either.

ARMAGEDDON

Evolution ran a little more than a year. There were a lot of highlights, a lot of good matches, especially as time went on. I had a good show with Bill

Goldberg, an Evolution run-in at *WrestleMania XX* that people still talk about, and some nice spots with Kane and Shelton Benjamin.

But maybe the biggest night for me came at *Armageddon*, December 14, 2003.

That was the match where I had my first really big single showdown with Shawn Michaels. I remember being in the ring first and watching him make his entrance. It was so surreal, it felt like a dream. It felt like I was watching TV. This is Shawn Michaels, a guy that I had watched and admired for years. The fact that I was there just didn't seem real.

Shawn Michaels was known as a great technical wrestler and heel well before he and Triple H launched one of the all-time great heel cliques, D-Generation X, in 1997. D-Generation X helped push World Wrestling Federation and wrestling in general in a whole new direction. Together with WCW's New World Order, D-Generation X helped make attitude an important ingredient of professional wrestling. Together with Stone Cold Steve Austin, D-Generation X helped bring millions of new fans to pro wrestling.

Recently, Shawn has been part of a resurrected D-Generation X, or DX as it's come to be known. A whole new generation of kids are turning on to our industry because of Shawn.

He and I worked a house show right before the Pay-Per-View, because he wanted to feel what it was like to be in the ring with me. I remember Shawn telling me that he was thrilled to death, because I was a big muscled kind of guy but didn't try to manhandle him inside the ropes. He was very surprised that I was relaxed in there. I learned something important from him that night, and it was like that lightbulb going on in my head that I mentioned earlier.

I'd always thought going into the "heat"—the point at which the heel really has his moment to shine, when he pulls some sort of nasty or dirty move and it looks like he might win the match—that the heat had to be a big elaborate thing: the heel has to hit somebody with a chair or kick him in the balls, do something really nasty and underhanded. But when I went in there with Shawn, I learned that the heat can be a lot simpler, and therefore more effective.

We were calling the match in the middle of the ring. I think we were in for two minutes when he said, "Shoot me off and give me a clothesline. Rip my head off."

So I shot him off and gave him a clothesline.

"What next?" I asked.

"Nothing. We're in the heat."

The crowd was with us, just on that simple move. He sold it, and then we turned it up. The crowd was so into things that we didn't need anything nastier. He sold what I did to him, and the more I hit him, the more they wanted to see him get into his comeback.

ME AND "THE MAN"

It was at that same *Armageddon* that I won the Tag Team Championship with Ric Flair. Even today, it's one of the highlights of my career. My name is linked with Ric's in the history books forever, which to me was like a dream come true.

The match was a Tag Team Turmoil match, which has two teams start off in the ring; once one team is down, the next team comes on. The Dudleys were the champs going into the match. There were six teams; we weren't on the original card. The Dudleys were the third team in, I believe, and it looked like they were the winners outlasting the others. But then Eric Bischoff—he was playing *Raw*'s general manager at the time—came out and announced that one more tag team was waiting for its turn. Ric and I came out and we flattened the Dudleys.

Believe it or not, not only was it the first time I won a championship, but it was the first time that Ric had won the World Tag Team title as well. It's hard to believe, since he's been around so long, but it's true. We held the title until March 2004.

You know what pops into my head sometimes when I'm talking to Ric?

I think, This is not real. This can't be real. I'm sitting here talking to Ric Flair, one of the greatest wrestlers of all time, and he's my friend. I won the championship *with* him.

Amazing.

IT CLICKS

Being in Evolution was fantastic for me. But my role was small compared to the other guys'. I think that at the end of 2003, the beginning of 2004, everyone was focused on Randy Orton as the future of the company. I don't mean that as a jealousy thing from my point of view, or to suggest he didn't deserve being looked at that way. Randy has got a hell of a lot of talent, and tremendous potential.

Maybe I was overlooked. But the fact is, I never really said much. I didn't do much. I pretty much set up guys for Randy or Hunter; that was my role. I'd have a big match with guys who would beat me and then move on to Randy or Hunter. I was just kind of in the background.

If I hadn't gotten better as a wrestler, if all those nights and mornings driving in the car and being schooled by Hunter and Ric and everyone else had been wasted, or their words pretty much had gone in one ear and out the other, if most of all I kept being afraid of being myself, then the odds are I'd have remained in the background. Evolution would have run its course, and I would have gone on quietly, I guess, staying on the edge of success, a guy with potential who wasn't *quite* good enough to command the limelight.

But then one night I went to Buffalo, New York, and had some fun.

Real fun.

And the world changed.

I can barely believe it: I'm the World Heavyweight Champion.

COPYRIGHT © 2007 WORLD WRESTLING ENTERTAINMENT, INC.

Moments after my win,
I "propose" to Angie.

Backstage with Zakk Wylde of Black Label Society.

COURTESY OF DAVE BATISTA.

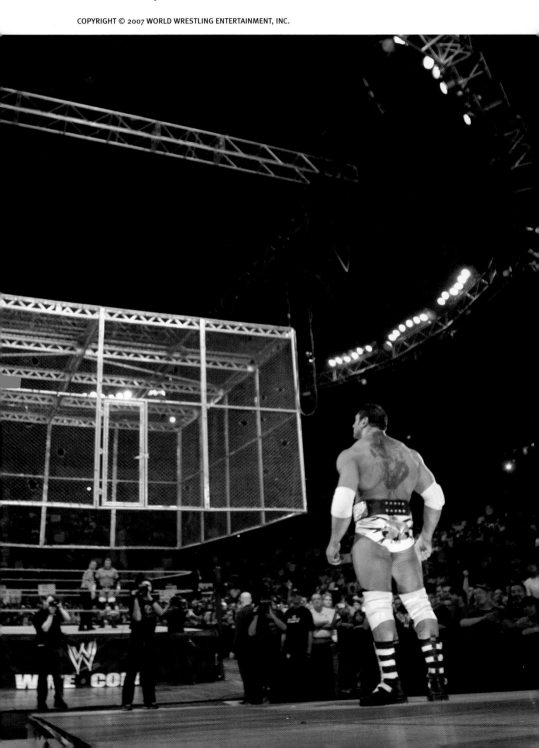

Hell in a Cell with Triple H at *Vengeance 2005*,
   one of my favorite matches.

COPYRIGHT © 2007 WORLD WRESTLING ENTERTAINMENT, INC.

Wrestling in Tokyo, one of my favorite places to tour.

COPYRIGHT © 2007 WORLD WRESTLING ENTERTAINMENT, INC.

We all still miss Eddie.

COPYRIGHT © 2007 WORLD WRESTLING ENTERTAINMENT, INC.

At *No Way Out 2007*, I remind Undertaker he has to beat me to get the championship belt.

COPYRIGHT © 2007 WORLD WRESTLING ENTERTAINMENT, INC.

Undertaker may have kept his
WrestleMania winning streak,
but I did not make it easy.

RIGHT © 2007 WORLD WRESTLING ENTERTAINMENT, INC.

FLASHBACK—
WRESTLEMANIA 21

Writing down my thoughts stirs up a lot of memories. One of the biggest highlights of my career so far has to have been *WrestleMania 21*.

It was at the Staples Center in Los Angeles, 2005. The place was packed to the rafters. Rey Mysterio defeated Eddie Guerrero, Edge won a Money in the Bank Ladder match. Undertaker pinned Randy Orton, Kurt Angle took Shawn Michaels. John Cena defeated JBL.

Some of wrestling's greatest stars from the past, including Roddy Piper and Hulk Hogan, shared the ring for the induction into the WWE Hall of Fame.

And then, it was our turn. Triple H and me, in the final event of the night.

The lights went down. Motörhead began playing "The Game" at the edge of the stage. Fireworks shot off. Triple H rose in the middle of the band, spitting water. The crowd roared over the music as he headed to the ring. Everyone was on their feet. The spotlights caught Hunter as he climbed the ropes, showing off his championship belt.

"Time to play the game," said Motörhead's Lemmy as the band ended their song.

The lights came up. My music started to play.

I came out onstage, walked side to side, bounced a few times, then headed down the ramp toward the ring. On the way, I paused and wiped a tear—a real tear—from my eye. I'd come so incredibly far in just a few years, from nowhere to headlining *WrestleMania*. It was just overwhelming.

Hunter waited in the center of the ring. As I climbed in, the crowd remained on their feet . . .

Five

CHAMPION

Evolution put my career on the fast track. But the road to my championship started unexpectedly, really by accident.

Within weeks, I was on a rocket-ship ride with only one destination: *WrestleMania 21*.

STEALING THE SHOW

November 22, 2004. Buffalo. *Raw.*

It started as a big joke. It was so trivial I can't even remember exactly why we did it. I think we were trying to get Hunter out of a match, give him a reason to take a break or something. And it wasn't even that big a spot. All I did was tease the crowd a little bit: Hunter gave me shit about a match and I turned on him, just a little, saying that maybe I wasn't happy with being in Evolution, and maybe I was going to quit.

The crowd was so sucked into it that by the end of the night they were chanting, "Ba-tis-ta! Ba-tis-ta!"

It was the first time I'd ever heard that so loudly. And it was a total accident. I just went out and had some fun. The more the fans reacted, the more I got into it. It seemed natural, even easy. Forget a lightbulb going on—the sun had come up in the middle of the darkest night.

At the end of the night, Hunter and I were laughing. We thought we'd fooled everybody. We figured we'd just go on the way we had been. But after the show, Vince called and said, "Man, it was your night. You stole the show tonight. That's awesome."

Hunter called, too. "We're so happy for you," he said. "That was great."

A VERY SLOW TURN

Over the next few weeks, we started playing with the animosity between me and Hunter. Just a bit.

It was a very slow turn. That was something the business hadn't seen in a while. It wasn't an overnight turn. It was very slow and deliberate. That was all Hunter's doing, too. He was really big on us not having a match until 'Mania. And by then, people were just dying to see it.

The ratings started shooting up as well. I don't really get involved in that, and I know it only secondhand, from other people. I could definitely feel the crowds pulling for me, though. While the conflict between Hunter

and me was building, the crowd was turning me into a babyface. They were cheering for me and just pushing everything in that direction. And the more they wanted it, the more possible it became.

Hunter is the one who believed in me enough to make me a star. He pushed me to the highest level possible. Hunter made me a star. He believed in me and he used himself to make me a star. I think Vince may have believed in me because Hunter believed in me, but Vince was good enough to take him at his word and hand me the ball.

I think I made the connection with the crowd somewhere at the point where I was afforded the right to go out and kind of be myself and not try to be a big bully brute. I'm just not a bully. I'm not someone who's always growling at people. I'm pretty soft-spoken and, I think, pretty humble and mild-mannered in real life. I'm huge, so don't fuck with me, but I respect people and try and treat them the way I'm treated.

Of course, push me and I'm on you with all the vengeance of a wild animal. Unleash my anger at your peril: that's what happens in a match.

I think the fans kind of connected to that somewhere and they just started taking a liking to me. Of course, I think too that the crowd likes it that I have an intensity when I wrestle. And I think the crowd's always partial to guys who are big and muscular. I think that's a common thing in our business. They've always liked guys who are big and muscular, like Hulk Hogan, Goldberg, Ultimate Warrior, The Warlord—big guys who can do serious damage.

At some point, not only did my showdown with Triple H become inevitable, but it became clear that we would be fighting for the title. And that I had a good shot at getting it.

A FUCKING KILLER

Nobody ever came up to me and said, "You know where we're going with this one." Or "We're going to do a title change at 'Mania." It's one of those things where you never really ask. You're afraid to ask, especially if like me at the time you've never had *the* title. You don't want people to think you want it too badly. Of course you *do* want it. But it's such an honor and a privilege to be in a main event of *WrestleMania*. So you just don't ask.

What you do is listen.

There are rumors and gossip, and just about everyone has an opinion. A lot of times it doesn't have much to do with anything based in reality, it's just words. But sometimes I'd hear some of the agents saying things like, "We're going all the way to the top with this one." Remarks like that gave me a sense of how real the run at the championship was.

I remember Arn Anderson was working with me and someone else one time and he made a point about how a match needed to be all about me. He said something like, "We're going all the way with this one, so this match needs to be right. He needs to look like a fucking killer."

Things like that fired up my hopes.

JUST A BLUR

The days leading up to *WrestleMania 21* are really blurred. I don't think I slept the whole week before the Pay-Per-View. On top of all the excitement and anxiety, I was having a lot of problems with my back. I had two bad discs in my spinal column. My left leg was pretty much numb. My sciatic nerve had been pinched or injured somehow. Not only was that really scaring the hell out of me, but I was having a real hard time training.

It figures, right? The biggest match of my career and I was having physical problems.

Finally, the day of *WrestleMania* came.

WrestleMania isn't just the biggest event of the pro wrestling world, it's one of the biggest events in the entire world. I've heard that more people see *WrestleMania* around the world than see the Super Bowl, and I can easily believe it. The crowds are immense, there are celebrities from just about every walk of life there, and the atmosphere is electric.

And then there's the television audience. It's huge in the U.S., of course, and it's just as big with our fans around the world. In the more than twenty years since it was started, *WrestleMania* has been the highlight of the sports entertainment year.

By slamming Ric,
I completed my
turn to face.

WrestleMania 21 was held at the Staples Center in Los Angeles, California. News reports said tickets sold out in less than a minute—which was a new record for the company. My match with Hunter was at the end of the night, but there was plenty of action leading up to us. Rey Mysterio and Eddie Guerrero had a terrific, terrific match; Undertaker extended his undefeated *WrestleMania* string by pinning Randy Orton, and Kurt Angle and Shawn Michaels gave the crowd a twenty-seven-and-a-half-minute show before Michaels finally submitted to a Kurt Angle ankle lock. John Cena defeated JBL—John "Bradshaw" Layfield—to take the WWE Championship.

And then it was our turn.

As I walked out to the ring I started having trouble breathing because I was so tense. The atmosphere was just exploding. Motörhead did Triple H's theme song live. The crowd was definitely into the show.

I don't remember a whole lot of the match, but I remember that right before I set Hunter up for the Batista bomb, I thought, "Oh my God, this is it."

Five years before, I was thirty years old and trying to start a career a lot of guys retire from at my age. Four years before, I was a big kid with a body and little else going for me as a wrestler. Three, two years before, I'd been a pro wrestler, but far from the big time. And a year ago, I'd been a guy so afraid of screwing up that I may have been headed for the discard pile.

And now I was seconds away from being the World Heavyweight Champion.

All I thought was, "I can't fucking believe this is happening."

I did my finish, pinning Hunter. The house erupted as we hit the canvas. I pinned Triple H, and I was the champion.

When I was handed the championship belt, I just broke down. A flood of emotions came out. I cried right there in the ring, for real.

DIAMONDS ARE FOREVER

All the boys and everybody was waiting for me when I got backstage. They were clapping. I was crying. They were smiling.

I mentioned earlier that I didn't do a good job when I proposed to my wife. It was half-assed, not the classy proposal she deserved. And we were so broke when we got married that we gave each other these cheap silver wedding bands, which she'd paid for out of her very small salary as a waitress.

Our circumstances now compared to then were as different as night and day. So before *WrestleMania*, I went out and bought her a diamond engagement ring from Tiffany's. I'd been looking for something nice for a while, and every place I went to said that they were second best to Tiffany's. So I said fuck this, I'm just going to go to Tiffany's. I want the best.

I gave it to Stephanie McMahon to hold and arranged for Angie to come backstage right after the match. When Angie met me, Stephanie slipped me the ring in its blue box. I had Hunter's blood all over me and it got all over the box as I handed it to my wife. She's probably the only woman in the world who got an engagement ring from Tiffany's in a box covered with blood.

She opened it and just started crying. I bent over her and I started crying, too.

Then I asked her if she would marry me, using the words I'd wished I'd used those many years before.

She kind of fell into my arms. It was a magical night.

A STORYBOOK CLIMB

I think it was special for the other people who were back there in gorilla with us, too. A lot of people took pictures. Shane McMahon gave me a copy of one he took. I still have it.

I also still have the bottle of Cristal champagne that Steph and Hunter gave us. We never opened it because that night I was so exhausted and in pain that we just went right to sleep. We wanted to save it for a special date. That date hasn't come yet, but hopefully it will.

That was my night, but I wanted it to be our night. Angie had been with me all along, I wanted to make it special for her.

Becoming champion was huge, but becoming champion at

This was it. I became the World Heavyweight Champion.

WrestleMania was even more special. And doing it by taking the title from Triple H—well, if you're talking storybook, it doesn't get any better than that.

I rose to the top extremely fast. I always tell people that Ric and Hunter put me on the fast track to becoming champion. If I hadn't been able to ride with them and pick their brains, I wouldn't have learned as much as I did, not nearly so fast.

The funny thing is, since I'd started so late, I was a lot older than most guys when I became champion.

I think that may have helped me in a way. You take a guy like Randy Orton. He started wrestling really young and became, I believe, the youngest World Champion ever. I think that was his downfall. He just wasn't ready for it He just didn't have the maturity and ended up having some personal issues that got a little out of hand. I would like to think that now he does have the maturity. Now he's older and you can see that he acts more in line with what the profession expects from a champion.

Frankly, I don't know how he did it at all when he was twenty-four. If I had gotten the title at twenty-four, I would have cracked.

PAIN

In some ways, I almost *did* crack in the weeks and months right after I got the title. Not because of the pressure of appearances and such, but because of the pain in my leg and back.

We went to Australia soon after *WrestleMania 21*, and it was there that I think that I finally broke down and got a prescription for painkillers. I had never used them before. It's not a regular thing for me, even now. I don't believe in them. I've seen guys get hooked on them, and I've also seen guys out of their mind on them. I don't want to be one of those guys in the ring with half his wits about him. If I ever become dependent on painkillers, I don't belong in this business.

The pain in my back was so bad that not even the pills the doctors prescribed could get it under control. When we came back from Australia, the doctors started on this treatment with epidurals in my spine to take care of it. The discs still bother me a little bit once in a while, but proper medication got it down to a manageable level.

THE COMPANY FACE

Football players joke that they're going to Disney World if they win the Super Bowl. A wrestler who wins at *WrestleMania* and becomes champion definitely doesn't go to Disney World—unless it's part of a promotion. One thing's for sure: he doesn't take a vacation.

What you do as champ is pack your bags and hit the road. You're suddenly in a lot more demand. You're the face of the organization, and you're expected to show yourself in as many places as possible. When other guys are having days off, going home and taking it easy, you're still on the road, doing interviews and appearances, and promoting this or that. Even at home, the champ ends up on the phone a lot, doing interviews for the media or whatever.

Being champion involves a lot more than just walking out into the arena with a big gold belt. You have to bust your ass in every way possible to fill up the arenas. Your job is to put asses in seats. You work harder, and at the same time, you have to keep yourself in top shape, because a champion can't look soft. No one can, but especially not a champ.

You participate more, even in backstage stuff, coming up with ideas and contributing to the show. You work with the younger guys who are coming up. You set an example.

I can't tell you how important leadership by example is in WWE. That's huge with us. I've tried to make my mark by remembering that.

I have to say, Ric and Hunter helped groom me for that stuff. I was definitely still learning when I got the job. But I knew what to expect. I knew the weight that would be put on my shoulders.

And I *wanted* it. I really did. I still do. I still want to be the face of this company. It's such an honor. Even after all this time, it's still an honor and a privilege. I don't mean to sound cheesy or hokey or anything. But there's a lot riding on the guy who's wearing the gold. The company is counting on you to carry that weight.

Greeting the fans
Down Under.

I accept that. It's why I'm in this business. I look down on anybody who doesn't aspire to be the champion. I don't even understand how they could even be in the business if they didn't want to be on top.

There are sacrifices, though. Your family takes a hit. It's hard to be a pro wrestler without some stress and strain on your family, some emotional injuries.

In my case, though, a lot of the wounds were self-inflicted.

CHICAGO, BOUND FOR OMAHA

I literally travel thousands of miles every week. The majority of times, maybe nine out of ten, things go pretty smoothly.

Maybe four out of five.

The bad times tend to bunch up, and after the Super Bowl Sunday show in Urbana, Illinois, they come in a pile. I'm traveling with Ken Kennedy and Bobby Lashley; we meet up at the airport and hit the only food place just before it closes, buying out the last of the tuna salad and nacho cheese dip. Kennedy has his fifth and sixth cans of Red Bull energy drink for the day, while Lashley struggles with one of the rudest airline ticket clerks going—and they're a rude breed—trying to make sure he's booked on the right flights.

Through security, we find out that our plane to Chicago has been delayed—a bit of a problem, since we have to make a connection there to Omaha.

There's nothing to do but wait. The plane shows up about forty-five minutes late, which happens to be exactly how much time we were supposed to have to make the connection at O'Hare.

We get up to Chicago just about the time our plane is scheduled to leave the gate. Our checked carry-on luggage is late coming out, and for nearly ten minutes we stand around shivering in a boarding tunnel so cold that Kennedy's hair freezes. Finally the bags come, and after following a maze out of the tunnel area we arrive at a gate right next to the one where our plane was supposed to leave from.

Here's a bit of luck—the plane hasn't finished boarding yet.

Two harried-looking gate attendants are handling tickets. Of course, all three of us head toward the cute-looking woman, Attendant No. 1.

When we get there, we find out that her computer seems to be rebelling, maybe because the flight is so damn late, or maybe because it had heavy money on the Bears and they're getting stomped in the Super Bowl.

Whatever, she works around it and somehow gets the machine to spit out boarding passes. For some reason Lashley gets four passes, but there are plenty of seats left open on the plane and the clerk tells him not to worry about it.

We shuffle over to the door, where Attendant No. 2 is living out his God fantasy by calling the names of the three people he managed to check in, anointing them with his blessing as he sweeps his hand toward the door.

Which he then closes in our faces.

"That's it. Plane is full," says Attendant No. 2.

"Well, why the fuck did you give me a boarding pass?" says a passenger standing with us. "What the fuck is going on?" (For the record, he wasn't a wrestler. And I'm toning down his language.)

Attendant No. 2 squints an Undertaker-like eyeball at him.

"What boarding pass?" he asks.

The passenger shoves it in his face.

"That other attendant just said there's plenty of empty seats. You got half the plane sitting here, waiting to get on."

Attendant No. 2 takes the boarding pass and holds it up to the light to make sure it's not counterfeit. He frowns when he sees that it's genuine, then goes over to the other attendant to confer. Smelling the possibility of blood—and having to get on the plane—we follow along.

After a short conference, Attendant No. 2 admits that the pass is genuine, but begins berating the passenger for not speaking up.

"What the fuck do you think I'm doing now?" says the passenger.

Attendant No. 2 ignores him, grudgingly stepping aside for him to pass into the plane.

"Who else has a ticket?" asks Attendant No. 2.

Along with the rest of the stranded passengers, we hand in our passes. Attendant No. 2 shuffles them and begins calling out our names. Things are going well until he gets to Bobby Lashley.

"Why do I have four tickets for this man?" says Attendant No. 2. "Where is this man, this Lashley?"

Lashley steps over to explain that there was a computer screwup, and that he only wanted the two seats he'd paid for. Because the seats on commuter planes are so cramped, a lot of us, myself included, will routinely pay for two seats; it's more comfortable for us and the people who would have to sit next to us on the flight.

But Attendant No. 2 isn't buying that explanation. No one in his experience would pay for two tickets, let alone show up with four. Now he is certain there is a vile network of boarding pass counterfeiters working in the airport. He is determined that they will not get by on his watch.

"No!" he shouts. "This cannot be! No four passes!"

"Well, it is," says Lashley calmly.

"What will you do with four seats?"

"I only want two," says Lashley. "Your computer screwed up."

"Computer does not fail," insists Attendant No. 2.

"It didn't fail, it screwed up."

"No, impossible."

"Don't mess with me, man," mumbles Lashley. "I beat up people for a living."

Unbowed, Attendant No. 2 shuffles through the tickets, lets everyone else on, then comes back to the four boarding passes with Lashley's name.

"This . . . this . . . is a problem," he says, ignoring Lashley completely. "Who is this Lashley?"

The other attendant finally comes over and provides enough of a diversion for Lashley to hustle onto the plane with us. The attendant tries to follow us on, but is kicked off the plane by the pilot, who's anxious to get to Omaha sometime this century.

The flight's good, the stewardess is really helpful, and things are quiet . . . until we land in Omaha, where we discover that our bags have not come with us on the flight.

Now, you know, and every person in America who has ever made a connecting flight knows, that the problem had to do with the fact that our plane from Urbana was late coming in. Either they messed up there in an effort to get the plane off because it was so late—unlikely but possible—or when we landed in Chicago they couldn't find a numb-nut smart enough to grab the half dozen bags bound for Omaha and walk them thirty-seven feet from one plane to another.

But the man at the baggage claim area believes a federal conspiracy is involved.

"We're only doing what the federal government allows us to do," he says when Lashley, who has media interviews first thing in the morning, asks if there's any way to have the bags delivered to the hotel very early. "Those bags may get here around nine a.m.—that's when the next flight is—but we're not allowed to deliver them until sometime between twelve thirty and four thirty."

"The federal government decides that?" asks Kennedy.

The man looks at him pitifully. Obviously, Kennedy doesn't understand the worldwide conspiracy.

"Well, why didn't the bags make it here in the first place?" asks Lashley, probably wondering if Attendant No. 2 decided to have them searched for a boarding pass machine.

"That happens because of weight restrictions," says the man with a straight face. "Very important, weight restrictions."

"With the bag or the plane?"

"The plane. When they're full, they can't take off."

"Ours was half empty," says another passenger.

"There, see?" says the man. "Too much weight and they can't take off."

Somebody probably ought to alert the FAA about that.

Six

THE LOVE OF
MY LIFE

There have been a lot of rumors and gossip and things about me and my now ex-wife, Angie, why we split up. A lot of bullshit, really.

It's not easy to be honest and open about what really happened between us. A big part of what happened has to do with me seeing other women—for a while, women became my drug o choice on the road. Some guys want alcohol or whatever; I wanted love. It hurts to talk about it, let alone to write it here for the world to see.

But I've tried in this book to be as honest and open as possible, and if I didn't talk about Angie, it would be like I was lying not just to you, but to myself.

Because really, she was and is the love of my life.

ANGIE

Before anything else, I should say that I love Angie. We're divorced now. Our marriage didn't work. This is my perspective on why. It's not meant to blame her, or even me for that matter. It's what happened.

I know that I've hurt her. The things that I did were not done to hurt her, but they did. Those things don't make me look good, but they're the truth. They're there.

Even good guys do bad things.

OUR FIRST TROUBLES

I think our problems really began because of the stress of my career, and Angie's insecurity.

It was really weird. I'd just started with WWE and I was on the road for the first time. People think that everybody they see on television is rich, but most wrestlers aren't. I sure wasn't. We moved back to Virginia from Ohio and right away started struggling financially. I wasn't making that much money—remember, I wasn't very important as far as the show went—but I had a whole batch of new expenses being on the road.

There's more than just travel. First off there's the hotels, food, and rental cars; the company usually only pays for airfare. There are dozens of little things. I mentioned the suit I bought earlier, for example; costumes are our responsibility. And then there are the expenses like gym fees and what have you. They all add up pretty quick.

Financial problems put a stress on any family. In my case, things were worse because I was rarely at home with my wife. I'd leave for

Me and Angie
at Hunter and
Stephanie's
wedding.

a house show Friday morning, then maybe get home Tuesday afternoon.

From Angie's point of view, I'm sure, it was as if she'd lost her husband. She went from having me home every night of the week to only seeing me a couple of days. And I mean "seeing" me: I would be so exhausted
that I never wanted to do anything, not even go out for a simple dinner or
a movie or whatever.

That made her a little bit bitter. We started having fights when I'd
come home. And then she became distant. It was as if she thought that by
not giving me her love when I was home, it wouldn't hurt her as much

when I left. Which never made fucking sense to me, because I would think that while I was home, she'd try to get as much love as she could.

I thought for a while that the fact she wasn't working was part of the problem. Her not working was a sore point with me. Not just because we were struggling—which we were—but I think she really needed to feel as if she was doing something important, for herself and for us. She really has a lot of ability and talents, and I think she—like all of us—feels better as a person when she's using those abilities and making a real contribution.

Angie's a really smart woman. She's also very caring. I think with that combination, she would be an excellent doctor, a pediatrician. I've seen her with kids and she really just has a way of comforting them that I think would make her a natural. She just has all sorts of abilities and I'd love to see her use them someday.

Anyway, Angie finally got a job. It was a bullshit waitress job. Her schedule was really close to nothing, a couple of nights a week, but it was something.

One day I came home early for some reason and she was supposed to be working. I called her at work, and she wasn't there.

"Wasn't she scheduled to work today?" I asked whoever I was talking to on the phone.

"Yeah, but she called in sick."

I couldn't figure out where the hell she was at. When she finally came home, she said she had been out boating with one of her friends all day. I just couldn't believe it. I exploded. I don't remember what I said, but basically I felt I was killing myself, we were struggling financially, and here she couldn't even go to work the few days she's assigned. Instead she's going out and hanging with a friend on a boat.

That was it. It fucking broke my heart. We split up.

JEN

While we split up, I started dating this girl who worked at one of the gyms I trained at. Her name was Jen and she was very cute, though a lot younger than me. She was a great girl.

One night Angie came over to the apartment that I'd taken and walked in unannounced.

I was there. Jen was there. And now so was Angie.

Of course, Angie just flipped. That, according to her, justified everything she had ever thought about me, that I was unfaithful to her all through our marriage, which was absolutely not true. But in her mind, I think, finding me with a girlfriend was really the final straw. Maybe if that hadn't happened, we would have worked our problems out. But now she thought that our whole marriage had been a sham.

She said she'd never forgive me for it. I don't think she has, either.

We stayed separated for a while.

CANCER

I don't know how much you know about cancer. At one time, it was basically a death sentence. People found out they had cancer and there really wasn't much hope for them. The only thing a doctor could really do was predict how long they'd live.

Now things are a lot different. The medical people know so much more about the disease now than they did even five years ago. There are a variety of different treatments, and being diagnosed with cancer is no longer a death sentence.

But . . .

But it's still a pretty devastating disease. (I guess to be technical, cancer is actually many different though similar diseases.) The treatments can really take a lot out of the patient, and even with the best medical care, there are no guarantees that he or she will survive. Prevention is a lot easier than treatment. Early detection and surgery are by far the best line of defense against cancer.

When you first hear that you or someone you love has cancer, it's heart-stopping. I don't care who you are or what you've done: if you have an ounce of emotion in your body, you think about what's important in your life. If you're smart, you rearrange what you're doing and make those important things your top priority.

ANGIE'S CANCER

Sometime in the spring of 2002, Angie started getting pains in her abdomen. At first, she didn't think they meant anything. They were just pains and she didn't give them much thought. But gradually they got worse, and finally she realized she had to see a doctor about them. The doctors ran a bunch of tests.

That fall or early winter, right around the time when Evolution was taking shape, Angie heard from a doctor that she had cancer.

I never went to medical school, so I'll leave the technical explanation to someone else. Angie had ovarian cancer. It started in her ovaries and spread to her small intestine. She also had cervical cancer, which is another type of cancer that affects a woman's reproductive system.

When I heard what was happening to her, I just had to be with her. I had to help her get through it. I just had to.

In a strange way, her getting sick got us back together and saved our marriage. It definitely put things in perspective for me. And not just about Angie and me. Up until then, I had given up on just about everything outside of wrestling. I didn't give a shit anymore about people, about a lot of things I should have cared about. I kind of didn't know which way I was going. But her getting sick really woke me up.

Angie went through radiation and chemotherapy. I suppose most people have heard about radiation—different types of radioactive material are used to basically zap the bad cancer cells. The basic idea in chemotherapy is similar. The patient takes very strong medicine that kills the cancer. In killing the cancer, the radiation and especially chemo do a hell of a job on the rest of the person.

It broke my heart to see Angie so sick. She lost so much weight. I think she says it was thirty pounds, but I'd swear it was more. And she was slim to begin with. She lost her hair. She takes so much pride in her hair, that had to kill her.

She's such a beautiful woman. She's so full of energy and life. Seeing her in bed, pale, wasted, maybe thinking that she wasn't going to be around much longer—it broke me in two. I would have gladly taken on her pain myself to spare her. I'd've gone through anything.

NO CHILDREN

Angie has been through chemo I believe four times now. It's never been as extreme as the first time she went through it, but it's not pleasant under any circumstances.

It's also very expensive. Fortunately, she was involved in a cancer study that helped pay some of her bills.

Cancer patients always have to worry about the cancer coming back. In her case, if it does come back, she's gonna have to get a total hysterectomy. That would rule out her having a baby. That would be a very big blow to her. It's something, unfortunately, she and I weren't able to do while we were married. I don't think there's anything in the world she wants more than to have a child.

Gradually, she got better. I remember we were doing some shows in Hawaii, and Angie and I flew out together early so we could be alone and relax and talk about our marriage. I can't quite recall now exactly when that was, but I can remember how great it felt to be out there with her.

I have to admit, though, we never did really repair anything that was wrong with our marriage, not in Hawaii, and not later. We kind of tucked our problems away. Angie was still convinced that I had cheated on her, not when we separated but before that and all through our marriage. And there was always that undertone of resentment in our relationship. It was like an acid, eating away at us.

PARTNERSHIP

I have to admit, the more she pushed me away, the more distant she got, the more resentful I became.

She didn't do anything for herself, in terms of a career or a job. And she didn't really contribute to the marriage in other ways. I wanted a partnership. I wanted someone I could share feelings with, and experiences; someone who would grow with me.

But even after she recovered from the cancer, she remained very distant. She blamed it on abandonment issues she had.

I think she used that as an excuse a little too much.

Once again, she started being very cold to me when I came home because she said it made it easier when I left. And once again, it didn't make any fucking sense to me.

The same issues we had before came up again and again. There was a lot of insecurity on her part. And I became . . .

What's the right word?

I can't find it. I guess the best way to say it is this: the more insecure she got, the more pissed off and resentful I got.

If she got insecure and accused me of doing certain things, I'd say, "Well, fuck you, I'm going out tonight and I'm going to party my ass off."

And I did. Which of course made things worse for her.

I got to the point where I always felt like I was a prisoner, like I was on a leash, and I would do things to prove to her that I wasn't her prisoner and I wasn't on a leash.

Stupid, stupid things.

I was an ass. And eventually, she was right to be insecure—I did start seeing other women on the road.

MY DRUG OF CHOICE

I'm not bragging. I'm not one of those people who cuts notches into a belt or anything like that. I'm not going to go into too many details since other people are involved. But to say it plainly: I started seeing and sleeping with other women.

I've confessed to Angie about it. She knows I was unfaithful to her.

It's one of those things I can't make excuses for. I did it and I was fucked up. I'm still not sure why I did it, because I was so in love with my wife. I still am in love with her.

Physically, we never had a problem. I know that for a lot of couples, there comes a time when they stop having sex, stop making love, or just do it very infrequently. It was never like that for us. We were always very sexual, very physical. The problems were communication and trust.

I know a lot of guys who had problems with drugs or problems with drinking. I've grown up with that my whole life. I think when you have a job where you're always traveling, moving around from place to place, constantly on the go without an anchor, maybe there's more stress for you. Maybe people, or at least some people, are more likely to have problems with drugs or whatever because of that stress.

I always thought I was lucky because I didn't have those sorts of problems. It took a while for me to realize that I had a similar problem with women.

I always tell people that I have absolutely no game with women. I don't know how to talk to them; I don't know how to pick one up.

My whole life before wrestling, and even up until WWE, I was shy around women. I'd only been in a few long-term relationships and didn't do a lot of dating at all before or between them. Then suddenly I was in a situation where women were throwing themselves at me. When I got on the road, I just wasn't prepared for it. I just had no idea how to handle it. It got pretty old real fast, pretty generic, not what I wanted. In that way, I got older and matured, but the damage as far as my marriage was concerned had already been done.

Angie said, Tell me and I'll forgive you. For a time, I didn't have anything to confess, and didn't. But then when I did confess to what I had done, she wouldn't forgive me. Just the opposite—she threw it in my face time and again, and never let me live it down.

A RICH GUY'S WIFE

The higher I got in the company, the worse she got. She started drinking, which didn't really help.

In 2006, I bought my first house down in Florida. I had gotten custody of my daughters—I'll tell you about that later—and had my mom come back east to live with us so she could help with the girls.

My mother didn't exactly know what she was getting into, I think. She was planning to come out for a vacation and I told her we were going to move to Florida. She was a little surprised, but she had a very good friend down there and thought it would be a nice place to visit. So she came and

The ladies in my life.

as soon as she was there she really lightened up the place. She's really special with the girls, and with me traveling, she volunteered to stay. I know it was a pretty big sacrifice for her—she really loves her life back in San Francisco—but her granddaughters were so important to her that she couldn't turn me down when I asked her to help out.

At the same time, things weren't going that well with me and Angie. Even after we'd been in the new house for a couple of months, Angie had not unpacked. She didn't do things around the house. Instead, she spent her time going to the gym, going shopping, having her nails done, and hanging out with her friends. She went out just about every night and partied.

I could not believe it. I was so busy; I was working my ass off, working so hard, and I felt she just wouldn't contribute to the marriage at all. It seemed like she had no interest in being there, or in me.

At some point, I began to think she'd turned into a bad stereotype: the bored, rich guy's wife. That's probably not the right way to put it—for one thing, while I'm not complaining, I'm not Bill Gates. But I think the stereotype is close enough to the truth. She became less of a partner and more like a token, a symbol: someone who doesn't do anything but look beautiful and spend money.

That's not what I wanted. That's not what she wanted, not what she was when we first got married.

Then at some point it got back to me that she had started bad-mouthing me. It was pretty negative. I was told that even when she saw people I worked with, she'd bad-mouth me, just rip me apart. She would tell them all the ins and outs of our personal lives, which just drove me crazy. Of course my friends would come running to me and ask why my wife was saying this and that.

I didn't know what to tell them. I couldn't hide how embarrassed I was.

At the last *WrestleMania* she went to, *WrestleMania 22* in 2006, she and I went out to an after-event party. I was dancing with her, and I was loving all over her. I was trying to physically show my affection for her—nothing X-rated, just dancing close and holding her the way a lover ought to hold the person he loves.

She just started getting really shitty, bitching at me at the party for some trivial thing I don't even remember. She walked away and went over to my mom, who'd come with us. She starting saying something about me—obviously, I wasn't there so I don't know exactly what it was—and my mother said something like, "What, are you kidding me? He's all over you. He's making an effort."

Angie told my mom that it was all a big act because I didn't want her to know that I was sleeping with somebody else who was there.

Basically, we'd gotten to the point where I couldn't even show affection without her thinking that I was only doing it to cover up, and hurt her even worse.

Pretty hard to have a relationship on that basis.

Our marriage had become this big, paranoid thing. It was ridiculous. She was really out of control. We split up for good not long after that.

As I'm writing this, we're in the final stages of getting a divorce. But the truth is, I still love her.

We're still very close. In fact, we talk every day on the phone and still see each other. She'll always be the love of my life. I just can't imagine my life without her in it.

I know it sounds strange.

At some point maybe we'll get back together. But I think until I leave this business, there'll never be hope for us. And I'm not by any means ready to leave just yet.

PURSUE HER DREAMS

As much as it hurts me, I think our being apart may be good for her. I think it may give her a chance to pursue her own dreams.

Angie has a lot of different abilities. She's very creative. She could have been a professional dancer, a singer, or both, if she'd pursued it. It always bothered me that she didn't. She actually did the national anthem for OVW and for WWE house shows, which shows you how incredible her voice was.

She's gone back to school and is studying to be a nurse. She'll be an awesome nurse. I said earlier that I think she can go beyond that and become a doctor, but whatever she decides, if she puts her heart into it, she is going to be the best at it by far.

Like a lot of people, she had doubts about how smart she was, even though it was obvious to others, especially me, that she was extremely intelligent. Maybe she can find that confidence by being on her own. I think it hit her one day that she hadn't done anything with her life over the last ten years or so. I think it sparked a fire under her ass. When she went back to school, she started to realize how smart she really is.

I am helping her go to school, and I'm very happy to play that small part. I have to say, I got a very easy divorce settlement. Basically, she just wanted me to help her continue her education, which is a lot less than she deserves.

Even though our marriage fell apart, I know I still love her. We can't be together right now, but what will happen in the future, I don't know.

HALFWAY TO SIOUX CITY

Arguing with baggage clerks is a waste of time. And time is something I really don't have tonight. It's just about midnight and I still have to drive from Omaha to Sioux City, where I'm due in the morning for *Raw* and some taping for the upcoming *WrestleMania*. Ordinarily, I wouldn't be on both shows—I'm a *SmackDown!* guy—but we're starting the buildup to *WrestleMania*, and my schedule over the next few weeks is going to get busier and busier. But I'm proud to be playing an important part in the show.

The luggage problem means I don't have any clothes except for what I'm wearing, but I do have my wrestling gear and championship belt. Those are always with me on a flight. Especially my championship belt. If I checked that, I'd be buying a new one every week.

I learned my lesson one time early on when we were doing a show in New Jersey. I forget where I was coming from, but wherever it was, the attendants wouldn't let me bring my carry-on inside the aircraft because the plane was just too small. So I did what they asked me to. I left it plane side.

where I guess it was supposed to be taken and then placed in the cargo hold. They guaranteed me that my bag would get there. Of course it didn't.

So I show up for the show, and of course, my gear is still up in outer space somewhere. I had to borrow gear from about three different guys to make up. I borrowed Randy Orton's trunks and turned them inside out. I got boots and a knee pad from Rodney Mac, and an elbow pad from someone else. It was all a little embarrassing. People still have pictures of me wrestling in Randy's trunks. They were turned inside out, but you could still see the imprint "Orton" on my ass.

From that point on, I've always kept my gear with me. I may not have my clothes, I may not be able to shave or brush my teeth, but I can go wrestle.

Tonight, Bobby Lashley volunteers to pick up my bags in the morning at the airport and bring them with him to Sioux City. With that straightened out, I head over to Hertz and grab my rental so I can get on the road again.

Lashley's a great guy, and a wrestler with a lot of ability—and I'm not just saying that because he's helping out. The first time I laid eyes on him I believe was up in Cincinnati. We were there for a match and a bunch of guys from OVW had come up. I saw Bobby Lashley and the thought "money" popped into my head.

The kid is just unbelievable. He's absolutely huge, he's intimidating, and he was a college wrestler, so you know he's got the legitimate background. He also wrestled in the U.S. Army, where I believe he was a two-time Armed Forces Champion.

Away from the ring, he's the sweetest guy going. But he's money inside.

I was impressed with him from that day. I actually begged Johnny Ace to get this guy on the road with us. You could tell he was going to be a world champion. What he's accomplished in a short amount of time is just incredible, and he's got a good future ahead of him.

Losing my bag wasn't the worst thing that ever happened to me travel-wise. All sorts of strange things happen on the road. Some of them turn out to be pretty funny—later on.

I once showed up at this hotel in Corpus Christi, Texas. They had my reservation, but somehow they booked me the wrong room: a smoking double.

I always get a nonsmoking king, because I don't fit in double beds, and if I sleep in a smoking room, my asthma flares up really bad. So as soon as I saw what they'd given me, I went back down and asked the lady at the front desk to change my room.

I should say—even if this turns out to be politically incorrect or something—the lady had one eye. Which was kind of weird.

She told me she didn't have a nonsmoking king and I kind of pitched a fit, telling her why I needed it. Well, finally she found me a nonsmoking king room. So I said fine. I went up and walked into the room, only to be greeted by a pretty fat naked guy who jumped up out of bed and said, "Hey, hey!"

I was a little upset.

I walked back down to the One-Eyed Lady and told her there's somebody in the room. She started arguing with me, telling me there wasn't.

"I'm telling you, I just walked in the fucking room, and a fat naked guy met me at the door. There's somebody in the fucking room!"

So she sent security up and the security guy came down.

"Yeah, there's somebody in the room," he told her.

So she found me another room. When I got up to the room, the air conditioner wasn't on. Now, this is in Texas, and it was during the summer, so when I say it was hot, it was hot.

I go to turn on the AC and the AC did not work.

By this point, I was getting pissed. I went back downstairs.

"I can't do anything," said the One-Eyed Lady. "We don't have another room."

"Then send somebody up to fix the air conditioner," I told her.

"Nobody's here. Just me and the security guy."

"So send him up."

So this poor older black guy comes up. He's just as nice as can be. But he doesn't really know much about air conditioners.

"Well, I don't know," he told me. "I just do security. I don't know if I can fix it."

He starts messing around with the wires and it kicks on. I'm like, "Great! I'm all set!"

I started thanking him, apologizing for being cranky and everything—when all of a sudden the AC catches on fire.

The security guy runs to the bathroom, gets a towel, and comes back. The wires were all sparking with flames, but he managed to beat out the fire.

I told him I was going back down to talk to the One-Eyed Lady and he better come back down with me, because it was going to get ugly. He was going to have to keep me from wringing her neck.

I went back down and I cut a promo on the One-Eyed Lady. She finally ended up canceling somebody else's reservation. It turned out to be a great room, with a king-size bed and a beach view.

I felt so bad later on that I tipped her and the security guy both a hundred bucks. And I apologized for being such an ass.

It sounds like a fish story, the One-Eyed Lady. But honest to God, there's not one bit of exaggeration in the whole thing.

Seven

SMACKDOWN!

WrestleMania 21 took place on April 3, 2005. I spent the next three months in the ring proving that I really was the champ, fending off various challengers.

It was a great three months. As a wrestler, I felt I had really come into my own. Some of those *Raw* shows may have been the best ever.

Reminding the fans, and J.R., that I earned the title.

Then, just when things were getting comfortable, WWE shook everybody up by changing the lineups for the company's flagship shows, *Raw* and *SmackDown!*

CHAMP

Every time a title changes, wrestling fans watch the new champion pretty carefully. They want to see if the new guy is really going to reign; in a way, they're trying to decide whether he's worth rooting for, and whether he's going to stick around. There have been some pretty short championships in this business. The new guy has to prove himself.

I didn't have a problem with that. I had some great matches. Randy Orton and I went at it on *Raw* right after *WrestleMania;* Kurt Angle and I tangled, and there was at least one good match in there with Edge that got the crowd on its feet from practically the opening bell.

But I think the most memorable shows were the ones I had with Hunter. We locked horns again and again. No champ likes losing the title, and Triple H kept coming at me. Our feud built to an incredible Hell in a Cell match that June at *Vengeance.* I still think of that match as one of the very best I've ever had.

HELL IN A CELL

That Pay-Per-View was the third time I'd faced Hunter. The Hell in a Cell format is fairly recent. A twenty-foot-high cell is erected over the ring and apron area. Once you're inside, there's literally no way out—the top is caged, and the door is locked. The matches tend to be vicious.

The most famous Hell in a Cell took place in 1998, when Undertaker and Mick Foley battled mostly on top of a cell at *King of the Ring 1998,* at the time one of World Wrestling Federation's Pay-Per-Views. That's the match where Undertaker threw Foley off the top of the cage, not once but twice. Undertaker swears he thought he'd killed him the second time. Every Hell in a Cell has that awesome feel to it.

I think a lot of fans expected me to lose the title at *Vengeance.* And looking back, I think that was the match where people started to look at me really differently. I think they decided then that I'm not a flash in the pan, that I really am a champion. It's not just a matter of who wins or loses a match or wears the title—it's the entertainment value of the match a wrestler gives. That's the sign of a champion. A champion gives fans a special experience.

At that match, Hunter and I took them on a ride, right down to the very end. I think right down to the very last second of that match, fans really didn't know who was going to win. And that's not easy to do.

Again, I have to give a lot of the credit to Hunter. He's such a talented wrestler, there was no way I couldn't look good. And in turn, his ability pushed me to elevate my work. He brought out the best in me, especially that night.

Hunter always got a bad rap for, uh, we'll call it hogging the title. He's been champ a lot during his career. The criticism was a really bad rap. Hunter was a champion so often because there weren't that many other guys who could carry the company like he could. It was one of those things where it was a necessity for him to hold the title for the company to survive. And he backed it up with his performances in the ring. He put asses in the seats.

Of course, that's just my opinion. I'm sure some people won't like it, or think that I'm sucking up to Hunter.

Too bad.

At the end of that match, I felt like I had arrived. There was really a huge difference between being the champion and being *the man*. And that match made me the man.

CALLING A MATCH

Thinking about that show brings to mind another great match that I had with Chris Benoit. I believe it was

January 3, 2005, on *Raw*, months before I got the title. I look back at it now as a milestone marking my career.

This, of course, was long before the terrible tragedy with his family. As I said before, the Chris who killed them and then took his own life was not the kind, unselfish man I knew.

The match was in Washington, D.C., my hometown. So even though I was a big-time heel at the time, half of the arena consisted of my friends and family, and I was really the hometown babyface. The match ended with a DQ, a disqualification, when I started just kicking the crap out of Chris and wouldn't stop.

The thing is, working with Chris, it was very easy to completely forget yourself. We always use the term "suspend your disbelief." People think of it mostly from the fans' point of view, where the fans are forgetting that it's entertainment. But it can happen with wrestlers, too. We can get sucked into the match and half think, half pretend that it's only entertainment. It feels real. Chris made it easy for that to happen. It's why he was so good.

I'm pretty sure Chris was the first guy to ever let me call a whole match. It happened before that *Raw* show, at some point when we were working together in house shows. I was still relatively new. He was the veteran, and for him to show that kind of confidence in me made me, well, it was pretty important.

Like a lot of wrestlers, Chris loved to call the match kind of on the fly because it made everything spontaneous and that much more real. He really liked to feed off the crowd. Plus he was such a talented guy that nothing could throw him.

I can't remember where we were that night, but I do remember him saying, "Why don't you call it?" I can see him as I'm writing this. He's got a little bit of a smile on his face. Not really a challenge, more like, "Welcome to the club, kid."

I was nervous as hell. I didn't want to screw up in front of Chris Benoit. I had never called an entire match to that point. But you know, it was an old-school rule: the heel would lead the match back in the day.

So I took my best shot. And it was an incredible match. And he was so fucking happy afterward. I earned a whole bunch of respect from him, and tons for myself in the locker room. If you earned Chris's respect, that went a long way. He put me over to all the agents, all the people in the office, even the veterans. Everybody. That was a big push for my career.

CHRISTIAN

Another good friend of mine whom I haven't had a chance to mention yet is Jason Reso—known as Christian. He helped me find my home in Tampa, which I really appreciated. I always loved working with him. On more than one occasion I heard Arn Anderson say he could watch Jay work all day—a pretty big compliment, coming from one of the best.

This is just my personal feeling, but I always felt like Jay was never really given his fair shot in WWE. He really had tremendous star potential. Maybe that's not for me to say, but I loved watching him work, and I loved watching and listening to him on the mike. He was funny, he was original—man, he had so much charisma.

I'll never forget the day he left the company. It was after a show in 2005. He came up to me and pulled me aside. He said, "I just want you to know I'm leaving. I'm not going to be here anymore."

He started crying. He was absolutely heartbroken, but he felt it was something he had to do. He felt like he wasn't going anywhere with WWE. His contract was up, and even though he'd been offered a renewal, he felt they weren't using him right and weren't likely to. So he left on his own terms. He went to a different company—TNA—which really gave him a huge push.

He was a good friend of mine when he was with WWE. Jay was one of those guys who didn't like to go out much—I don't know if he didn't like to or he just wouldn't because his wife wouldn't put up with it. He'd have just one drink and then be out of there. But no one ever held it against him because he was so much one of the boys. He had a lot of locker-room respect. We felt his absence for a long time. I hope one day he'll return to us. I think he's a hell of an entertainer, extremely underrated when he was here.

STARTING OVER

Not too long after *WrestleMania 21*, we started hearing rumors that the company was thinking of changing the lineups on *Raw* and *SmackDown!* I heard they were toying with sending Hunter over to *SmackDown!* And then there were rumors about me going over. Finally I went to Vince and asked him directly.

"Are you moving me to *SmackDown!*?"

"Yes. We're moving you to *SmackDown!*" he said. "We're counting on you. This is your show."

That may sound flattering, but to me it felt like I was starting over. And I walked into a locker room that didn't like me very much.

Some of those feelings came from an interview I did earlier that year. The interviewer was talking about the competition between *Raw* and *SmackDown!* asking which brand or show was better, that sort of thing. I was a *Raw* guy at that point, and so I was speaking up for my show. The thing is, I did it basically by ripping *SmackDown!* I really did put them down—pretty much ripped them a new asshole.

There were some guys on *SmackDown!* at the time who in my opinion didn't work as hard as they could. I dogged them out.

Part of the interview was taken out of context, but the truth is I didn't say anything I didn't mean. I was being prideful and I thought I was representing our show and saying, "This is why we're better."

Now remember, I had been on *SmackDown!* Some of the guys there were more concerned about where they were going after the show than with the show itself. There were some guys who were very content with their spots. They didn't want to move up; they just wanted their five minutes on TV because that was enough to go out and get them laid.

I thought I was being smart at the time by not naming any names, even though the interviewer pressed me. I think I talked about guys being lazy bastards and not showing pride, that sort of thing, but I didn't name anyone by name.

CALLED OUT

Most of the people I was referring to in those interviews have long since been fired. But the problem was, by not singling anyone out, I seemed to be criticizing everyone over there. Which I hadn't really intended on doing.

It's funny, but I don't think I realized it until Undertaker came up to me later and asked if I'd said what was printed in the interview.

"Yes I did," I told him.

"Well, that's fucked up."

"Why?"

"Well, let me fucking tell you why." And he explained—I have to say very reasonably—that I had left the door open for everyone to think I was referring to them. And that plenty of readers would think that, too.

Undertaker was very good about this, because he could have been a total asshole. But he made me understand what I'd done wrong.

"Are you telling me there's not guys on *Raw* like that?" he asked.

"Yes, there are. But we weren't talking about the guys on *Raw*. We were talking about *SmackDown!* I was just thinking being competitive."

"Dissing us and being competitive are two different things. You were dissing the company, not *SmackDown!*"

I don't have his exact words here—it happened too long ago—but his meaning was pretty clear. Even though we're on different shows and we're competitive, we're still part of the same company. Everyone in WWE has the same goal. Putting someone down in the media pulls the company down.

"If you have something to say, or you want to light some fire under our asses, you go to the guy and tell him. Directly," said Undertaker. "That's what being a leader is. Bring this shit up in the locker room. Don't go to the goddamn press and put it out there. We got all these guys who are very talented and working their asses off and who think you're dogging them, for no reason. You're just setting yourself up to be a target."

It was good advice. The whole incident was part of a learning experience about how to deal with the media. I didn't understand how the press might twist your words around just a little bit, or not add in a question, or take part of your answer and put it in the interview. It's hard to be careful about the little parts when you're focused on the whole. I think I'm a little better with it now, but of course, the damage had been done.

GIVING SHIT

That conflict was definitely playing in the background when I went over to *SmackDown!* Another thing that didn't help was my relationship with Hunter. There are a lot of guys in the company who don't go for him, and if you're his friend, they take it out on you. He'd warned me and Randy about that before we starting riding with him.

I don't want to name anybody personally, but at the time we had a few of the old veterans who believed highly in hazing and giving rookies shit. I wasn't a rookie anymore, but they didn't think that the guy who's only been in the business a few years should be champion, and they made that pretty clear. It was very hard for me to start over there.

I think things have changed somewhat since then. I think I've earned some guys' respect. Vince once said to me, "You're going to get a lot less problems from guys if you're putting asses in seats." Which is true, though even then there can still be an undertone of resentment. But I think for the most part, people know that I'm not an ass. I have the same goal as they do: I want our show to be number one.

I'm very prideful about *SmackDown!* I hate to hear that *Raw* has higher ratings than us. It's a matter of pride.

OIL AND WATER

People have asked me why I think Vince decided to make the change in the shows. I think there were a number of reasons, but I don't think the controversy about my comments had anything to do with it. I don't think he thought there would be more heat because of them or anything. I do think he thought I would do good things for the show, and that John Cena, who came over to *Raw* from *SmackDown!*, would be good for *Raw*.

I also think that the move was intended to get me a whole new range of opponents. You know, really, I had started with Hunter, basically at the top. There wasn't that much else for me to do but work my way down. I don't mean that as a knock on the guys who were there; I'm looking at it from the viewers' perspective. I think from their perspective, I would have had no place to go but down. That would have diminished the character I'd worked so hard, and everyone around me had worked so hard, to create.

Put me on *SmackDown!* though, and it's like starting from scratch. I

Not only can he drink, the man can talk.

got a whole new bunch of guys to work with, and it doesn't seem to the fans that I'm going backward.

My first feud was with Bradshaw—JBL.

There's a whole generation who are going to know him as a commentator and even a financial advisor, but John "Bradshaw" Layfield has had a great career in the ring. Back in the late nineties, he teamed with Faarooq to form the Acolytes, who were a pretty popular tag team. After that, Bradshaw was part of Undertaker's Ministry of Darkness and in 2002 held the WWE Hardcore Championship belt, which he named the Texas Hardcore Championship, in keeping with his character. He was a big, big arrogant Texan, good at riling up the crowd.

You would think, two big guys like us, the matches ought to be great. But for some reason we didn't have very good chemistry. We were like oil and water. We struggled, and I could never quite figure out why. I almost think that sometimes you get a much better match when you have a mismatch between the wrestlers: you know, a bigger guy and a smaller guy. Or contradicting wrestling styles.

I have more of a brawling style and so does JBL, so maybe that was the reason we didn't quite click. We tried, but it just didn't take off.

Not to say we didn't have tons of fun. I'll tell you, he's a funny son of a bitch to work with. You get him on a mike, and he's very entertaining.

He's funny even when he's not trying to be. One time he'd been on vacation somewhere for a week or something. I swear while he was gone, he put on twenty pounds. He came back and we were doing our match. I went to lift him up for a suplex—a move where you pick up your opponent and drive him into the ground with your own body. I started straining right in the middle of it. Twenty pounds can make a hell of a difference.

"You're heavy," I told him.

"I've been on vacation."

Anyway, we went through the move and I got him upside down and we're starting to fall and he just started yelling at me, "I've been on vacation! Take it easy! I've been on vacation!"

I hit the mat and started laughing.

JOHNSON CITY, TENNESSEE

I've had a lot of fun with JBL outside the ring.

There was the time when we were in Johnson City, Tennessee. I can't remember now, but I think we might have had a match with each other that night. There was only one place in town to go after the show. It was kind of a redneck bar. I happen to have some good buddies there; one of them is a deputy sheriff, Anthony Nelson. So we were in this place—it was pretty big, and crowded; I think everybody in town was there that night. I was sitting over on the restaurant side and eating with my buddies. JBL and Orlando Jordan were over at the bar drinking. At some point, they started sending drinks over to the table.

"Fuck," I told my friends. "This is JBL, calling me out."

So we finished eating and walked over. I started ordering shots for JBL and Orlando, like twenty at a time.

JBL is pretty good at beer—he can sit and drink beer all night. But once he starts on hard liquor, it's downhill pretty quick. I was ordering Grand Marnier, Jäger shots, and Goldschläger. That's the stuff that really gets you.

Bradshaw is funny in general, but he's a really funny drunk. He was making fun and just got us all laughing. But after a while, I started seeing him dry heaving.

As soon as I started seeing him dry heaving, I ordered thirty shots, forty shots. I swear to God. We got the whole bar wasted. Those Tennessee boys can really drink.

Orlando was smart enough to sneak off. He went over and started singing karaoke and hanging out. We tried to keep calling him back, but he was just too smart.

The next thing you know, Bradshaw—who by this time was sitting on the bar—started puking. As he was puking, I was handing him shots. He kept drinking them. He's puking and drinking, puking and drinking. He never said enough is enough. He's a fish with no cutoff mechanism.

The place was such a redneck bar that when he started puking on his stool, people looked over, said no big deal, and looked away. They went right on drinking.

That was a Sunday night. JBL and I had a dark match on *Raw* the next night, so we had to catch a flight out the next morning. He showed up at the airport green. I was still so drunk I could barely get dressed.

I called my wife that morning at six, trying to explain why I hadn't called her that night.

"Baby, I was out with Bradshaw."

Oh, that went over big-time. I don't think she spoke to me for a week.

We flew into Pittsburgh. We were supposed to be at *Raw* at one in the afternoon. Orlando—he's the guy who wasn't drinking that much, remember—felt so bad he had to call for a car to get him to the arena. I don't know what time John showed up—it was earlier than I did—but I got there about ten o'clock.

As soon as I got there, I walked into Vince's office and told him, "I'm the drinking world champion of the world."

I told him the story. Now, some girl had told me—I never confirmed it—that JBL was so drunk he peed in his pants. I told Vince that. I said I didn't see it, I didn't witness it, just that some girl had told me that. And I told him, Now don't tell John I told you this, it's all between you and me.

Well, we had to take the corporate jet that night. I forget where we had to go but Vince was there and I was and JBL was as well. So we get on the jet and it's real quiet, and all of a sudden Vince goes, "So what's this I hear about someone getting so drunk they pissed their pants?"

He threw me right under the bus.

One of the best nights of my life.

EDDIE

From Bradshaw, I started to move into a thing with Eddie Guerrero.

It started in the fall of 2005, with a bit where Palmer Cannon named Eddie the number one contender. I did a tag team thing with Eddie and we slowly built up some heat between us. Then we had a title fight at *No Mercy*, the Pay-Per-View that October. That was the show where I led the crowd singing "Happy Birthday" to Eddie after we went dark, which was kind of a nice moment, because all of the fans gave him a really warm ovation.

I'd actually met Eddie years before when I was at OVW. We had gone up for a match in Cincinnati and he was there. I don't know exactly what he was doing, whether he was coming back from an injury or just helping guys out. But I met him up there for the first time, and he was very gracious, very helpful, and that was my first introduction to him.

Soon after I came over from *Raw*, Eddie and I were doing a show in Columbus, Ohio. We both happened to be backstage when I got a call that my daughter had just given birth to my grandson, Jacob. The doctors said there was something wrong. My daughter's blood pressure had shot up dangerously high, and there was a problem with the baby as well.

I broke down right there, in front of Eddie.

He asked me what was up and I explained.

"I can't believe that you never mentioned anything," he said, or something like that.

I didn't want to mention it. I was afraid what people were going to think. My sixteen-year-old daughter was having a baby. What kind of dad was I, that my daughter was having a baby that young? It was really something that I hid. I didn't bring my personal problems to work.

But Eddie, without hesitation, went to his bag and grabbed his Bible. He opened it up and had me read this passage that he had memorized.

It was about people judging people. It was beautiful. I can't remember which passage it was, but it basically said that no one has the right to judge you, and that you can't live your life according to other people's judgment. Only God can judge you.

It fit that moment just perfectly. It made me feel a lot better.

"GO TO YOUR DAUGHTER"

"Right now, you need to go be with your daughter," Eddie told me.

I was afraid to ask for time off. I'd also been having problems with my daughter, and I wasn't sure exactly what to do about them. I didn't know if showing up would be the right thing.

Eddie insisted.

"Just make a call," he said, telling me to call WWE management and

Jacob.

explain what was going on. "Just go be with your daughter. You're no good to us here with the way you are. You need to go see her."

We did our match and I made a call to Johnny Ace, the head of talent, and I told him what was happening. He was very supportive. He had the company put me on a plane to go see my daughter and make sure she was okay.

And to meet my grandson.

I took my first look at him and fell instantly in love with him. I hadn't seen my daughter in months—I'll tell you about some of that later—but all my anger and bitterness just disappeared when I looked into that little boy's wrinkled face. Things were changed. The baby was there and there was nothing we could do about it. I wasn't ready to be a grandfather, but he was ready for me.

In that moment, I realized that the only thing that was important was that baby. And that it's important to try to forgive and forget and move on from there.

Eddie really, really opened my eyes to that. We were tight from that day on.

EDDIE HAD MY BACK

He also watched my back. A couple of times that I had problems, he was there. One time I came back from my match and one of our security guys pointed me toward the locker room and said a bunch of the guys were waiting for me. When I went in, a bunch of the top guys, all the vets, were there. They started laying into me about a problem they had with me.

It's trivial now, though of course it didn't seem quite like that at the time.

I had been seeing this girl on the road and brought her to a couple of the shows. The guys had problems with that. They thought it reflected poorly on them and were concerned what their wives might think they were doing.

I told them fine. I understood. They'd never see that again. That solved the problem.

Eddie was there, not to judge me but to make sure things didn't get out of hand. I know he was ready to defend me if it became necessary. Stuff like that meant a lot to me.

We used to travel home together a lot, because Eddie lived in Tampa at the time, and we had some pretty good talks. We'd talk about the angle we were running. He put a lot of thought into it and was really excited about working with me.

Eddie knew I hadn't been in the business all that long. He knew I was still green, still learning on the job. But he always made me feel like a champion. He would always call me a thoroughbred.

"You're a thoroughbred," he'd say. "You're pulling the chariot right now, and we need to all get behind you."

He never made me feel like I was a rookie, or anything less than a world champion. I always loved Eddie for that. Even though he was a veteran and had been around forever, he never made you feel like you were less than his peer.

He was also the kind of guy who never passed judgment on anybody. He'd made a lot of mistakes in his life, and he never forgot that. He never forgot where he came from, or what he'd been through, and I think that helped give him a certain perspective on things.

Of course, that's not to say when you were out of line, Eddie didn't let you know about it. Eddie was one of those guys who was never, ever—not to anybody—afraid to speak his mind. And I respected him for that, too.

LAUGHING THROUGH THE PAIN

The thing that always amazed me about Eddie Guerrero, and that you'll hear from every guy you meet, is that Eddie was always in pain. He had back problems and he was always really hurting. But as soon as he walked through that curtain, it all went away. He was intense, he was funny, he was energetic. And those vignettes he did—he could make you laugh, he could make you cry, he could make you hate him, he could make you love him. He was just so talented.

God, he was a funny son of a bitch. Keeping a straight face working with him was impossible.

I guess every fan is going to have their own favorite bit. I used to love this thing Eddie would do where he would piss an opponent off and then drop down on his knees, like he was praying. He'd kind of crawl around and hug your knees. It was just hysterical.

One time he had a match with Undertaker. While Undertaker was making his entrance, Eddie made a show of trying to hide behind one of the posts. He really had a knack for physical comedy. He turned simple bits like that into hysterical gags. He was a great showman.

THE WATCH

In November 2005, we had an angle going where he was trying really hard to gain my respect. We were working to a point where he would stick it to me with a really hard heel turn. Which was where things would have really started picking up and getting interesting. He had all this funny stuff planned out.

One show was going to be centered around him stealing my watch. He was going to do this thing where he noticed my watch in one segment and he'd say, "Ah, that's a nice watch! I've got one just like it." Then, next segment, I'm looking for my watch. I wouldn't be able to find my watch. Then he would come in and he'd have my watch on. But he'd say, "Hey, what do you think? Here's my watch. It looks just like yours." And of course, it's falling down to his elbow.

"Are you sure that's not my watch?" I'd say.

"No, no, it's my watch, man."

Then a segment later, I'd get my watch back, and he'd accuse me of stealing *his* watch.

The routines would have gone on from there, until I stole his clothes and car and left him naked in the parking lot. It would have been hilarious.

Eddie was real good at things like that. He would be the butt of the joke just to entertain you.

THE CALL

On November 12, 2005, my wife and I were in Minneapolis, staying at the same hotel that he was in, the Marriott. We were all going to Europe for a tour. She was coming with me, and we were planning to leave from the hotel.

Eddie called me that night, pretty late. I think it was about two in the morning. I was already sleeping, so he left a message.

At the time, I was champion. The plan was to pass the title back to Randy. But I wanted them to put it on Eddie. I'd told him earlier that I was going to Vince to ask him to do that.

Well, Eddie called me and left a message saying that he really appreciated what I was going to do, but that it was the wrong decision. Randy should be champ, not him.

"We should do what Vince says. Vince is smart," said Eddie. "He knows this business, and he wouldn't make a wrong decision. It's what's best for this company."

He's promising to support me, but I know you can't trust Latino Heat.

He added that he loved me and appreciated that I wanted him to have the title, even though it was the wrong decision.

I got up later that morning. My wife started going through her messages and all of a sudden she started crying. Dr. Rios had called to tell us Eddie had died.

I just couldn't believe it. I just fell down. I was in disbelief. My wife and I both started crying. I think I cried for a week straight.

Everybody did.

But we still had to go and do the show. *Raw* and *SmackDown!* were having a supershow, where we were working together. Everybody was just heartbroken, absolutely in shock and heartbroken. There wasn't a dry eye in the building.

TEARS FOR EDDIE

That show, I drove Eddie's lowrider in. Eddie always used to drive it in and make it bounce. But when I drove it in, for some reason, the hydraulics wouldn't work. There was no bounce. It was as if the car were in mourning like the rest of us.

They wanted me to do an in-ring promo, to talk about Eddie. I told them I felt funny about doing it. Eddie and I weren't longtime friends like he and Chris Benoit were, and we weren't family like him and Chavo were family. I thought they would have been better choices.

Eddie meant a great deal to me, but I didn't have the history with him like those guys and a few others in the company did. I felt funny going out, because I didn't think I was the right guy. But I went out and did it, because I was asked to, and because Eddie deserved it. I was really emotional. I got into the ring and I was already in tears.

I was heartbroken, and right away some smart-ass in the front row yells, "You suck!"

I ignored him. "I don't know if I'm the right person to be out here speaking about Eddie," I said.

The same guy goes, "You're not."

He was just being a smart-ass, trying to steal the spotlight at a completely inappropriate time. We were in real mourning and this guy's just being a fucking asshole. That's the kind of guy I wish I could catch after the show so I could just beat the living shit out of him. There'll always be assholes like that out in the world, but sometimes you just have to shut them the hell up.

I hope he dies a horrible death. He's a piece of shit in my book.

TRIBUTES CONTINUE

I don't think I have recovered from Eddie's death. I don't think anybody has. I see his wife, Vickie, every once in a while. She still participates on our shows. She's not over it. I see the kids all the time. They lost their father. I know they're not over it.

You know, it doesn't feel like we *lost* Eddie. It feels like he was ripped right out of our arms. It's still shocking. It still hurts.

A lot of fans still mourn him, too, around the world. We see signs remembering him, honoring him. Things like "Eddie Guerrero Latino Heat," and all the signs you used to see people holding up when he was still with us. I always, in some way, shape, or form, in every match that I do, give a little salute to Eddie. I think some people pick up on it. I hope they do, and remember him.

And then in a lot of ways, he's still with us. A few matches ago, Kennedy wanted to do this thing where he slapped me, then dropped down on his knees. And I said, "That's so Eddie-ish." And then he started imitating Eddie and we just started laughing and telling stories about the funny shit Eddie used to do.

He's still with us in that way. He'll always be.

The *Raw* show in Sioux City, Iowa, went pretty well Monday night. It started with a bit where Undertaker chose his opponent for the upcoming *WrestleMania*. You could hear the crowd hold its breath as he made his choice by choke-slamming me to the canvas.

It was strange being on *Raw*. I hadn't been there in a while. Right before I went out, I looked at Michael Hayes and said, "I hope they'll remember me."

"Oh, they'll remember you," he said.

It's weird, but you do worry about things like that, at least I do. But the crowd gave me a really loud welcome, and that felt really good.

But that was last night.

Now it's Tuesday, and I have to be in Omaha, Nebraska, in a few hours for *SmackDown!*

I'm running late. I climb into my rented car and program the GPS unit to get me back on the highway. Mentally, I'm already changing gears, getting ready for the show.

Kennedy and I have a big match planned for tonight. It's

a Street Fight, which means it's going to be physically brutal, and I have to gear myself up for that.

I also have to get there on time. The GPS gets me onto the highway quickly. With the road nearly empty and the pavement straight, I step on the gas and go.

Eight

COLLATERAL DAMAGE

After Eddie died, I started working into a thing with Mark Henry, "the world's strongest man." Just a few weeks into that, I was injured at a house show. Mark hurt me when he did a move I had no idea was coming.

Mark's got a good heart, and he didn't intentionally try to injure me. But it doesn't take away the fact that he was careless

YOUR HANDS, MY LIFE

When you're in the ring with someone else, you're responsible for that person's well-being. You have to protect them.

What that means for a wrestler is that number one, you don't do anything that will hurt them. You shouldn't take chances for yourself, but there's a very sacred tradition that you don't take chances for someone else. The other guy's life is literally in your hands. You always let them know what move you're going to do. And you don't experiment. If you have a new move that you want to bring into your act, you work on it under controlled conditions, at a workout or practice. While a certain amount of wrestling has to be spontaneous, you don't want to blindside somebody with something they're not expecting. The regular moves are dangerous enough.

We communicate in the ring. That's a huge part of what we do. We have to communicate in there, or someone could get killed.

On January 6, 2006, I was doing a house show with Mark Henry. At some point he set me up for a move I think he calls the Chocolate Moose. Or "mousse," however the hell that's supposed to be spelled. I don't know whether it's a dessert or a big deer or something you do to your hair. Maybe all three.

Anyway, he did it without telling me. I never saw it coming because I had my back to him. I trusted him. Maybe that was a mistake on my part.

Mark had been out for a while and I'm positive he hadn't done that move since he'd been back. Which to me means he shouldn't have done it then. If I'd known he was going to do it, I would have said no way. I wouldn't have let him experiment on me, certainly not in that situation, in a house show.

He hit me with his full body weight. He slammed me to the canvas and my arm exploded. It took the entire weight of the move, tearing my triceps, the same one that had been injured before.

I was obviously in a lot of pain, but we kept going. Mark hit me with the ring bell and the ref called it a DQ. He left the ring and I was kind of recovering. Then they had him come back down and I picked up everything I could and hit him, just so I'd be leaving with the crowd cheering. I think the first thing I hit him with was the belt. Then I picked up the stairs and hit him with the stairs.

I was running on pure adrenaline. Even though my arm was hanging off my shoulder, I still picked up the stairs. But I was hurting. And mad.

I didn't hurt him with the stairs or anything else, of course. But I can't tell you how upset I was. We were getting ready for the *Royal Rumble* and headed into *'Mania*. I was holding the title at the time. I felt he was completely reckless. We try to give our best in all our matches, but he took me out for a long time. He took a lot of money out of my pocket, a lot of money away from my family. And the injury took a lot of money, I believe, out of the company. I still to this day can't figure out what he was thinking.

Mark's got a good heart, and like I said, he didn't intentionally hurt me. But it was still careless.

SURRENDERING THE TITLE

I knew it was torn right away. The company wanted to send me down to Birmingham, Alabama, to see Dr. Andrews, who is one of the best orthopedic surgeons in the world. He does repairs for tons of professional athletes, and a lot of guys in our company.

First, though, I had to go in and surrender the title. I didn't want to, of course—no one wants to give up anything they've worked hard to earn, and the championship belt meant a lot to me. If you have to give up the title, you want to do it in the ring, during a match. But of course, it had to be done; I was going to be out of action for a long while, and there was no way I could wrestle until after I had my surgery.

I turned over the title on *SmackDown!* in a very emotional show. If you find a tape of it, you'll see I was very choked up. I was in Philadelphia, and I left that city in tears. I really did.

While I was on the flight down to Birmingham, Alabama, to see Dr. Andrews, he had a heart attack. I had no idea when I walked through the door the next morning. His assistant met me in the hallway.

"Did you hear about Dr. Andrews?" she asked. "He had a heart attack."

"Well, who's going to fix my triceps?"

It's funny now, but I guess it wasn't the most caring thing to say. I did go over and pay him a visit that day in the hospital, just to see if he was okay. The funny thing is, he sat right up in bed and examined me there. He wasn't going to let a little thing like a heart attack slow him down.

As a matter of fact, he yanked my arm around pretty good. That guy is tough as nails. He's a great guy.

His partner, Dr. Jeffrey R. Dugas, fixed my arm. He was one of the best doctors I've ever had, and not just as a surgeon, stitching me back together. He called me all the time, just to see how I was doing, to check up on me. He was very careful. They were very worried about me getting an infection, because the tear was in the same area that I had injured earlier. I guess when you cut into scar tissue, you can have some serious complications later. I couldn't even go to a gym—not even to say hello—for at least a month. They didn't even want me sweating.

They fixed it by taking a piece of my hamstring out of my leg and weaving it into my triceps. The repair I have in there now is so strong it feels better than it has in years.

REHAB

I was out for just over six months. I moved to Birmingham for a while and went through rehab there. I was fortunate to work with Kevin Wilk, who I believe is one of the best physical therapists in the country. We did a lot of simple exercises, stretches, a lot of rotator cuff work, and different things to keep my body from getting stiff. A lot of what I did had more to do with trying to stay in shape than with rebuilding my shoulder.

You wouldn't believe it, but rehab was actually a lot of fun. There was an all-star cast of athletes working out around me, trying to get back in the game. It was one of those places where you wish they had cameras set up— it could be one of the best reality shows ever. We all went out collectively a few times. Birmingham's a small town, so you get a bunch of pro athletes walking into a place and it's like the Red Sea parting for you. They treated us like kings pretty much everywhere we went.

Drew Brees, the NFL quarterback, was in there rehabbing his shoulder. He'd been playing with the San Diego Chargers but I think had just entered free agency, so there were guys down there trying to recruit him. It seemed like every pro team was in there kissing his ass. We gave him a bit of ribbing for that. Drew's a good dude; I wish him the best. Some of the other football guys I hung with were Freddie Mitchell, who used to play for the Philadelphia Eagles, and Will Demps, who at the time was playing with the Baltimore Ravens and now is with the New York Giants. Both those guys are great guys.

Get a bunch of jocks telling stories, and it makes for an entertaining day. Then guys get to ragging on each other, and man, that's pretty funny, too. It takes a little of the pain away from the work you have to do to get back in shape.

I met Charles Barkley, the basketball legend, while I was in Birmingham. Barkley used to train at a Gold's Gym there. I was there working on some of the cardio equipment upstairs. This huge guy on a stationary bike started waving at me, telling me to come on over. So all right, I walked over. I didn't realize who it was until I was about three feet away. Then I recognized him and I immediately turned into a little kid. I can't tell you how many times I saw Barkley on TV when he was with the Sixers or later with the Suns. I actually admired him for getting into fights, sticking up for his team.

He started talking to me like he knew me. I mean, I've always been a big Barkley fan, but to have it turn out that he was a Batista fan—that's just very surreal. Very cool.

ALONZO MOURNING

Speaking of Charles Barkley, I met another of my basketball heroes thanks to wrestling, though I can't say that he was much of a Batista fan. In fact, his idol turned out to be Triple H.

The player was Alonzo Mourning. He's best known now as a star for the Miami Heat in the NBA, but back at the end of the eighties and early nineties he was starting for the Georgetown Hoyas, then as now one of the country's top college basketball teams. Seeing as how I was from Washington, D.C., Georgetown University was my local team and I was a big fan of theirs and of Mourning.

Hunter and I did a celebrity pool tournament at the tail end of 2004. The only thing I remember about the tournament was the fact that Alonzo was in the celebrity tournament, too. I, of course, turned into a little kid. I was just about jumping up and down. "Man, it's great, it's Alonzo Mourning, yeah!" I was thinking to myself.

Anyway, Alonzo saw us and recognized Hunter. He came over and started talking to him, telling him he's a big fan, the whole thing. Hunter thanked him and they started talking.

I have to admit, I was kind of jealous. Here's this guy I absolutely idolized, and he was talking to my friend for a good half hour and pretty much ignoring me. I just kind of stood there, taking it all in.

So, they're talking and talking. Finally, Hunter says good-bye to him and we all move on. As we're walking away, Hunter turns to me and says, "Who was that, anyway?"

"Are you fucking kidding me?" I asked.

"No. Who was it? Really. Who was it?"

MR. POTATO NOSE

That sort of thing happened a lot that night. People would come up to Hunter and he had no idea who they were. He has tunnel vision sometimes. If it doesn't involve wrestling, he doesn't know about it.

We were at that pool tournament the day after I'd broken my nose in Seattle. One of the pro pool players there was Jeanette Lee, who is among the best women pool professionals in the country. I had a huge crush on her—still do. Anyway, I got to meet her but I was so embarrassed because my nose looked like I'd been on a weeklong coke binge. It was a real potato. I was absolutely mortified, meeting this girl who was the hottest thing in the world. I was married and wouldn't have asked for a date anyway, but I still would have liked to at least look, uh, human. Instead of Mr. Potato Nose.

"HE'S STILL HOT"

Hunter has all sorts of fans across the world. As a matter of fact, my mom is a great fan. She calls him a living legend.

Mom also loves Rey Mysterio and she was a big Eddie Guerrero fan before he died. She likes Vito. One time we were doing a shoot or an interview or something down near my house, and she made us all dinner. She was going on about how handsome Vito was; I thought I might have to keep my eye on her. And Kennedy—she was saying just the other day that she felt real bad when people were booing him at one of the shows.

In 2006, she came with us to a party at *WrestleMania* where a lot of old-time wrestlers as well as current stars were. She went up to Mae and Moolah—that's Mae Young and Lillian Ellison, who is better known as the Fabulous Moolah—and had me pose in a picture with them, because they were among her all-time favorite "girl" wrestlers, as she calls them. And she still talks about meeting Sherri Martel at the Hall of Fame dinner.

"She hasn't aged a day," she whispered after she met her.

But probably the most fun for me was introducing her to Ric Flair. She's been a fan of Ric's for many years. So when we were all at a party together, I decided to take her on over and introduce her to him.

"Mom, I want you to meet somebody," I said, and I kind of steered her toward Ric.

Her mouth dropped open. Ric was his very charming self.

"Oh, what an honor!" said my mom. "I'm a big fan."

"Oh, no, the honor is all mine," said Ric.

"No, it's not! You don't know."

"No, really, the honor's all mine."

"No, really, you don't understand!"

They went back and forth like that for a while. I had to do my best not to burst out laughing.

"You know, he's still hot," said my mom later. "He's still hot."

"I WANTED TO SLAP HER"

Taking my mother to a show is a lot of fun. I'm just sorry I can't sit out there and watch her. But I get reports.

A lot of times she'll go out with signs. One time in San Francisco when I was still on *Raw* she got in trouble. I guess the local security people didn't realize she was my mom. She had this two-sided sign. One side read "Batista is *Raw*" and on the other side she wrote "I love Batista." So they were trying to get her to put it down or move or something because she was blocking the view or a camera.

She told them, "I'm sorry. I was just excited because I was going to see my son wrestle."

The security people started apologizing all over the place, but she put her sign down anyway.

Of course, if your mom's in the audience, she may take things a little personally. There's a story about her being at a show and this woman nearby yelled, "Hey, Batista, when you get old, you're going to be ugly!"

Supposedly someone had to grab her and keep her from slapping the woman, but my mom says that didn't happen.

"I *wanted* to go over and slap her," she said when I was working on this book. "But I thought, That's not a very nice thing to do. It wouldn't reflect very well: Batista's mom being dragged out of the place because somebody said when he got old he's going to be ugly. I wanted to say we come from a really pretty good-looking gene pool. I didn't, though. But I did want to whip her. I truly did."

That's her version and I believe her. But if I were you and I was sitting near her at a show, I'd be careful what I said.

FAMILY BUSINESS

I have a very supportive family. I can't say enough about my mom, how really strong she is and how still, after all these years, she's a big part of my life, and the lives of my children and grandchildren.

Michael at his high school graduation.

I haven't had a chance yet to mention my half brother, Michael, my father's son from his second marriage.

I was worried about this kid when I was younger. My father and his second wife were kind of stiff and anal so I thought Michael might turn out to be a snooty little prick. Their house was always spotless, they were so uptight about everything. They were a typical yuppie couple. They made me want to just stick my finger down my throat. When he was little they'd dress him up just so, make sure his shirt was always tucked *perfectly* in his pants, have his hair combed every second. If they gave him a cookie, he always had to have a napkin with it and couldn't get crumbs on anything or make any kind of mess without getting in trouble. I really did think he was going to be an anal prick.

But the opposite is true. He's amazingly cool and easygoing. He's got it all. He's smart; he's athletic. His high school football team, which he was a part of, was Virginia state football champs.

When Michael was around one, maybe even a little older, even though I wasn't living at the house anymore I would go over and babysit for him. He was such a cute kid. Right off the bat I loved him. Unfortunately, we drifted apart because of the problems I had with my father. There came a point where I hadn't talked to my dad and his family for so long that they told me Michael didn't believe he had a big brother—I think he was convinced they were making me up, because he hadn't seen me in so long. But somewhere in there I started going over again and seeing him.

We really started getting close as he got older. I think our sister, Donna, really encouraged it. She had stayed in touch with Michael as he was growing up and really let me know I should, too. When he was in his later years of high school we started hanging out a little bit. He's a social kid—he's so social he can hang out with my friends.

Which ended up not being a good thing: I don't know if I should give him up, but he'd ask some of my friends to buy him kegs and they'd do it. He had the neighborhood party house for a while. He was even hanging out with us in nightclubs when he was seventeen, eighteen, holding his own with my friends. That's pretty impressive—my friends are veterans in the nightclub scene, they've been around for years and years.

I remember one party I had for the boys—I try and throw parties for everyone at WWE every time we're in D.C. for a show—and I invited my brother. It just so happened that he ran into a girl there who used to go to the same high school that he did. She was a few years older, and there with a friend, but he ended up with both of these girls on the couch.

At one point I looked over and he had his arms around both of them. They were snuggling a little bit, and maybe there was a little bit of kissing going on. I was so happy my face was glowing. I said to my wife, "Look at my little brother. He's just mackin'."

"Yeah, just like his big brother," she said with a not very nice attitude, and kind of walked away. Which kind of tells you where my marriage was heading at that point.

Michael's in college now, with a real bright future ahead of him. He's the kid I would have dreamed of being when I was younger: successful, athletic, personable. I'm just so proud of him. I'm very proud to call him my brother.

MY GIRLS

As I mentioned earlier, I have two daughters by my first wife—the only good things that came out of that marriage. I love them both very much. At the moment that I'm writing this, one is sixteen and the other is fourteen.

Three years ago, I went to court to get custody of them. I was alarmed by what was going on with them and their mother. She'd become verbally abusive and wasn't providing, in my mind, a very good atmosphere for them to grow up in. I decided that I had to try and give them a steady life, some sort of direction and consistency. I owed them at least that, as their father.

I'll spare you the real ugliness of the court process. It's not easy for a guy to get custody of his kids. There's still a pretty big prejudice against fathers in that respect, regardless of whether they're celebrities or not. And in my case, having a job as a professional wrestler didn't exactly help my cause. A guy standing in front of several thousand fans and asking them whether to pulverize an opponent or not doesn't exactly project a nurturing image. We all had to go through pretty extensive psychological evaluations before any decision was made.

I should mention the attorney who helped make my dream of winning back my children a reality. Her name is Rebecca Masri and she is awesome. I owe her a lot. She looks like a sweet little Jewish girl until she enters the courtroom. Then she morphs into a Louisiana pit bull.

The whole court thing tends to focus on the parents rather than the well-being of the kids, or at least it can seem that way. Their mother tried to make out what a bad person I was, turn me into Mr. Evil, just the most horrible person in the world. I was fortunate that in the end, the courts considered the situation fully and decided that I could provide a good atmosphere for them to grow in.

Athena, the youngest, still lives with me. I have to give her a lot of credit. She's constantly on the principal's honor roll. She's class president. She's starting a really prestigious prep school next year. When she was a little girl, she said she wanted to go to Harvard. Now she seems a little more focused on UC Berkeley. Whatever school she chooses, I know she's going to succeed there. She's got her head on so straight it's scary. I truly believe that young woman is going to achieve great things in her life. I am really going to enjoy watching her grow. I'm so proud of her, I can't begin to put it into words.

It's heartbreaking to say this, but my older daughter, Keilani, and I have really drifted apart. It seems odd, because we really had an early bond. I used to take her with me to work out at the gym when she was still in a baby carriage. Some of the happiest moments of my life, especially in those days, came when I was with her. It's funny: all those old clichés about not appreciating what you have until it's gone really turn out to be true.

On the other hand, my youngest daughter and I never really had a lot of that time to be together when she was tiny. I was already out of the house when she was a baby. Even though I was always close by and made a huge effort to be in both my daughters' lives, I didn't live with Athena when she was a child. I thought that would have made a bigger difference than it has.

But it's just the opposite. Athena and I have a very strong, solid bond. She has absolutely no communication with her mom; she won't speak to her, let alone have anything to do with her. My older daughter really worships her mother.

JACOB

Keilani got pregnant during some of these court troubles. To make a long story short, we agreed to let her stay with her mom until after she had the baby. Then we'd go back to court. We had moved to Florida, so we had to travel up to Virginia, where they lived, to get everything settled. After the baby was born and the court made its decision, she moved down to Tampa with us.

My grandson, Jacob, is really an awesome little kid. I know all proud fathers and grandfathers will say the same thing about their children, but my guy is definitely special. You see his little smile and you melt. He's just a special little boy.

Unfortunately, it wasn't long before my daughter was in trouble again. The court gave us custody of Jacob, hoping to provide him with a little consistency and security in his upbringing.

It takes two to make a child, and Jacob's father was a young man named Ricky. Ricky tried hard to be a good dad. The only negative thing about Ricky was that, though a couple of years older than my daughter, he was still pretty young. But he was a good kid at heart. He wanted to be in the baby's life, and he was willing to do whatever it took to be there. You have to admire a young man with that kind of responsibility and desire to be a father.

We helped him move down to Florida and found him a place to live, even got him a car. We gave him and my daughter some commonsense rules, including some about sex—basically, we didn't want them to create another child. I don't think for a minute that our rules were very popular, but they were necessary.

Unfortunately, soon Ricky and my daughter started having really bad problems. She had started a new school and, I think, was interested in another boy. You can imagine the mental trauma.

Ricky started pushing the rules and doing things that he really shouldn't have been doing. But he started really flipping out when my daughter wanted to split up with him for the new boy. He came over one night and locked himself in the room with her, and threatened to take the baby away.

I wasn't there, but my mom was, and she banged on the door and yelled at him to open up. Eventually, they called me and I talked to him on the phone. I wasn't very nice—I was pretty much an asshole—but I was trying to protect my daughter and grandson. I was afraid that he was acting psycho.

Finally, things calmed down. Angie was there and helped. I told Ricky, "We'll do anything to help you be a father, but we have to have rules." He wasn't ever allowed to disrespect my mother, or to come over the house when I wasn't home. I told him straight, the reason was that I was afraid he wanted to take the baby.

Unfortunately, he decided he wanted to move back to Virginia. I can understand the trauma and anger he was going through at the time, so it's hard to blame him. He needed some separation from my daughter, and that meant he had to leave his son, too. That part of the decision had to be very, very tough for him. It must have really hurt. He was the one changing diapers, playing with him, feeding him—a lot more than my daughter did. Before things became such a big problem, Ricky would take Jacob on overnight visits to his apartment. He was such a good dad. Anyone could see how much he really loved his son.

But he did what he had to do. He moved back to Virginia. And not too long after that—just a few weeks, it's all a blur now—I got a call while I was waiting to make a connection at an airport. Ricky had died in a car accident.

God.

I have tears in my eyes as I'm writing this. It was so unfair. He was such a good dad, and had so much potential in life. And the flip side is the loss for Jacob. He's just never going to know his dad.

It breaks my heart.

FUNERAL

At Ricky's funeral, people were given a chance to speak. Not a lot of people had seen Ricky with Jacob and I wanted to just tell everybody how much he really loved his little boy. I never stood up and said anything because a lot of people blamed me for chasing Ricky out of Florida.

I regret that.

People thought I made him move out of Florida, which couldn't have been further from the truth. I brought Ricky to Florida. I paid for his apartment and car; I gave him extra cash when he needed it. I encouraged him to be there. I was very supportive of him. I just wasn't willing to let him hurt my daughter or make her life any more stressful. It was unfortunate that it got like that for a while.

I told him I'd help him be a dad as long as he wanted to be. But he couldn't handle the rejection of my daughter, and that was the reason he left.

I'm hoping someday Jacob will read this and know that I loved his dad. His father was very special and truly loved him dearly.

MORE TROUBLES

Unfortunately, the problems with Ricky didn't help the situation with my older daughter at all. She ran away again and, though I don't know how she managed this, got married. Because of that, we lost custody of her, even though she was still only sixteen.

It gets worse. Her marriage meant that we lost custody of my grandson as well.

After she ran away, her mom and I managed to locate her and got her to meet us at the airport in Florida. She'd taken Jacob with her, and we expected that when she returned he would be there, too. But he wasn't. Both her mother and I became very upset that she didn't bring the baby back. She flipped out again and started to run away.

We thought we were lucky because we were able to get some police to help us when we explained that she was running away. But after the officers spoke to her, they came over and gave us the bad news.

"Your daughter's married now," said one of the cops.

"Yeah, we heard," I said.

"Well, in the state of Florida, your daughter's now emancipated."

Basically, that meant she was no longer in my custody. Neither I nor the police could tell her what to do.

We got a court order that said she was supposed to bring the baby back home. My first wife made the mistake of taking the baby and hiding him, which ended up with her getting arrested for not complying with the court order.

I know this is getting a little hard to follow, so I'll cut to the ending: we got Jacob back, but only for a month. In the end, the fact that my daughter was emancipated trumped everything else. My grandson went back to her. And in the meantime, she's had another kid, Aiden. I love him a lot, but unfortunately I haven't had much contact with him.

I love those little kids. I pray that they're going to be okay, and I'll do anything I can to make sure they are.

LOVE RUNS DEEP

I've always told Keilani this: I love her unconditionally. I'll always love her.

I'm more than a little pissed off at her, though. I'm not really pissed off at her because she got herself pregnant and had two babies, or dropped out of school. I'm pissed off at her because, for one, she never came to me and said, "Well, I did this. I messed up." She just ran away.

And two, she always treated me like the enemy when I was the constant in her life. I was always there for her. I never judged her. I always told her I loved her, and I've felt like her mother did the opposite. I always felt like her mother wanted her to choose one of us. With me she never had to choose. She could still see her mom. I wanted her mother to be a part of her life.

I tried to offer her the best life she could have. I don't know what she was running away from. I was never physical with her, or my other daughter. I never even raised my voice. When they were little, I didn't have to.

She had everything she could want. I still can't figure out why she was so mad at me.

I guess most people might think, Well, he wasn't there when she was little. But I think that I've always made an effort to be in her life.

Someday maybe these wounds will heal. Someday I hope love wins out. Because I deeply love my daughters, both of them. And my grand-children. It's unconditional, and it's forever.

OMAHA

I make it to Omaha in world-record time and pull around to the back of the Qwest Center, where the security guys are already waiting for me. I park the car and head backstage to check in with Michael Hayes and make sure everything's ready for the show tonight.

Somewhere in here I should mention Nicole Dorazio. She works in talent relations and she makes my day-to-day life as easy as it can possibly be. She handles all my travel and scheduling and is a very good friend and confidante. She's also become a very good friend of my mom's. I don't think I could get through a day without her, especially one like today where I'm doing so much traveling and having the right connections is absolutely essential.

Typically we do three house shows a week, and the last day of the tour is always our TV day. That's a long day, because we always have to show up to the ring very early, about noon, and we don't get started with the show until seven thirty or eight. Even later with *Raw*.

We spend a lot of the day sitting around, kind of waiting.

It's one of those days when they have catering, so there's always food around, which is hard. You have to fight to stay away 'cause it's usually not very healthy food. If you're bored, it's real easy to fall into that, you know, pigging out on junk food all day.

But TV days are really a down-to-business day. You can be sitting around one minute, and then hard at work the next. It's kind of the calm before the storm.

The pretapes—the little vignettes that air between wrestling matches—are shot on TV day. We try to get them done in one take, though a lot of times that's impossible. You just keep working at it until you get it right.

At the same time, guys will try to get in the ring to get their workouts done. Sometimes you'll see guys running steps in the arena, trying to stay in shape. Especially on a day like today, when it's really cold outside.

Once my taping is done, I put on some sweats and go out into the ring. The production people are working their butts off. I think a lot of times the boys take the backstage people for granted, because they don't actually see the work they put in. I know I do. But when you think about it, they're already there before we get there, and they tear everything down after we leave, so they're working even longer than we are. They're spending their lives on the road, away from their families just as much as we are.

The production crews function like a well-oiled machine. These guys don't miss a beat. A lot of the crew guys have multiple jobs. They drive the trucks, and they'll put up the ring, and then they'll have a role in the show. Take Tony Chimel, who's the *SmackDown!* announcer. Every night, he's the guy setting up and breaking down the ring. He comes in, he puts it up, changes into his suit, and announces the show, then he puts on his sweats and breaks down the ring. A lot of our refs do that, too. They double as crew guys. They travel on the crew bus and they're going around the clock.

The talent guys aren't the only characters in our company. You have to travel with the camera crew sometime to see characters. They're true-blue characters. Hysterical. They've got some stories.

One of the referee/production guys who I'm close to is Charles Robinson. He's been very good to me. Sadly, his wife passed away from cancer. He knew Angie was going through chemo, and we shed a lot of tears together around that time and became very close. He's one of those guys I love on a personal level, not just as a professional.

Man, he's a hard worker. All of them are. Charles goes in, sets up and breaks down the ring, refs matches, and in between he's taking photos for us.

Our crew members are great. One of these days, I'll bet they'll get together and write their own book. I just hope they're kind when they talk about me.

Nine

BACK ON TOP

I had a really strong desire to become WWE Champion, and an even stronger desire to become a man people in the company looked up to. Those are awesome responsibilities, and I wanted them, as heavy as they might seem.

After I got injured, my desire to make it to the top the first time was nothing compared to my desire to get back there. I guess that's one thing about leadership. You don't stop proving yourself.

COMEBACK

I rehabbed my triceps for a couple of months in Birmingham, then eventually got to the point where I was able to go home. There I worked to get back into shape and maintain my edge. I'd go back periodically to the doctors and the Birmingham rehab, where they'd check me out and see how I was coming along.

Finally, I was ready. I was really psyched to come back, but the company had to pick the right spot. And the spot they picked was the place where I'd left off: Philadelphia, where I'd surrendered the title.

I have to admit, when they told me that, all I could see in my mind's eye was me walking out of the building, teary-eyed. I was nervous going back there. Philadelphia's a very tricky crowd. They don't like mushy babyfaces. Philadelphia is a city of fighters, tough guys, and they don't like crybabies. I was afraid that's what they were going to think of me as—a crybaby.

People don't realize it, but I'm an emotional guy. It's who I am. And I was afraid the people in Philadelphia were going to misinterpret that.

I was wrong, though, very wrong. They're tough, but boy, those people in Philadelphia—you get them behind you and you can do anything. The place just blew up when I walked in. It was as if each fan were telling me individually to get back in that ring and take what was rightfully mine. When people are behind you like that, you really want to perform for them.

I called Mark Henry out and you could feel the tension in the building. The crowd loved it. They were really sucked in. Forget about suspending disbelief—they were practically writing the show for me. Mark walked out and I gave him a good old-fashioned ass-whipping and that building just went nuts. I think the walls are still vibrating. It was my night: July 7, 2006.

What's mine is mine.

HENRY'S TURN

I knew Mark Henry and I were really going to have a real good thing. The injury, the revenge angle, it was really going to work. We were just getting warmed up.

But then, less than a month later, Mark blew his knee out. So that ended that.

Mark's injury sent us scrambling for a couple of weeks, trying to come up with a new story line. They threw me into a quick thing with Ken Kennedy—Mr. Kennedy. It was a transition, just to get something going until me and King Booker hooked up for a title chase, but it was a sign of things to come with him. As I've said, Kennedy is really a good worker and I think he has a good future with this company.

Some of the matches I had with King Booker in those few weeks didn't go all that well, and things were a bit awkward until Booker and I finally got on track. Whether the fact that there was a bit of real heat between us helped or not, I don't know, but people have certainly speculated on it.

KING BOOKER

Booker and his brother Stevie Ray first came to national attention as the tag team Harlem Heat on WCW in the mid-1990s. Back then he was known as Booker T. As a solo wrestler, Booker won most of WCW's titles, including the WCW Championship, which he held five times.

He came over to World Wrestling Federation in 2001, after our company bought WCW. Since then he's been involved in a number of important matches and feuds, starting with an attack on Stone Cold at the *King of the Ring 2001*. He began calling himself King Booker after defeating Bobby Lashley at *Judgment Day 2006*. A big part of his act as "king" is the very gorgeous Queen Sharmell Huffman, his wife. Outside of the ring, both are very involved with charity and other causes; they do a lot of good things for people. Together they have a foundation called Booker T Fights for Kids, which sums up what they're about.

Booker and I had had a falling-out the spring before my comeback. We were in L.A. to do a photo shoot for *SummerSlam*. We got into a disagreement that escalated into a fistfight.

A real fistfight. It wasn't part of a promo or anything like that.

King Booker had become champion while I was gone, and I think in his opinion I didn't give him the professional courtesy or respect that any veteran wrestler, let alone the champion, deserves. Which was true. I showed up at the photo shoot and I pretty much said hello to everybody except him.

I had a personal problem with Booker, which was why I was rude. People have pushed me to talk about the personal aspects, but I don't care to go into it. We move ahead. And the point is, no matter how I felt, I should have at least been respectful and said hello, not acted as if he didn't exist. He's earned respect in this business. I didn't show it, and I was wrong.

Anyway, one thing led to another and there we were in a fistfight. Kind of silly. But that's where it ended. The next weekend, Johnny Ace—John Laurinaitis, the head of talent—set us up together for an appearance. The real reason he wanted us there was so that he could be there and make sure we talked. And we did. I apologized to Booker for not giving him the respect that he had earned. And that was it. Our problems were pretty much squashed after that. We decided we were both going to be professional and put our personal differences aside. We really have the same goal, the betterment of the company. We had to work like professionals, have some good matches, and try to make some money with each other. Which we did.

It wasn't easy. There was still a little bit of personal tension between us. I think that Booker was hell-bent on showing people that I wasn't the star that he was.

But that didn't last very long. We started having fun out there, and all that personal stuff and grievances went right out the window. We started having fun with each other, and there were some real good matches. Real good matches.

REAL HEAT

There's a perception out there that if two wrestlers have some real disagreement between them—if there's real heat like there was between me and Booker—the matches are better. But the opposite is true.

When people actually have real disagreements or dislike each other, their shows usually don't do very well. It comes back to the need to trust people, I think. And the fight in the ring depends on both guys working together to make each other look good, so you have to be on the same page with that.

Plus, when fans know that two guys actually do have disagreements or personal problems with each other, they're expecting so much violence, they're bound to be disappointed.

Matches are always better when wrestlers are on the same page, if they're clicking and they have one goal in mind. That goal isn't to show the other guy up. Because it takes two really excellent performances to make the show really click.

I don't think you have to love each other. Booker and I, we'll always have disagreements. We're always going to be—let me put this politely—two different people. But we can still get in there and have fun working together. I believe I have earned some respect from Booker, and I definitely have given him the respect that he has earned and has a right to after all these years in the business.

THE BIGGEST-DRAW BULLSHIT

One of the things that preceded my dispute with Booker were rumors that I was going around saying that I was the biggest draw in the company, that I was carrying *SmackDown!* and WWE on my back. Booker threw those rumors in my face, and it really pissed me off.

I didn't say anything like that. I didn't think it. I don't think it. I don't even wish it.

But you can deny something over and over, and it just keeps coming back, for whatever reason. Maybe some guys want to believe the worst.

Those words have never come out of my mouth. Not anything even remotely close to those words came out of my mouth or ever would. Because really, that would be disrespecting Hunter, disrespecting Ric, disrespecting Shawn Michaels, disrespecting Undertaker, disrespecting every other wrestler in the company, not to mention guys the public hasn't heard of because they work behind the scenes. I'm just not a piece of shit like that.

The opposite is true. I'm one of those guys who sometimes wonders how he got to the big time. I know my limits. I'm not extremely talented. I'm terrible on the mike. I have physical limitations.

Where I think I've had success is in using what other people have taught me about wrestling, about working the crowd. Things I've picked up from Ric on how to tell a story in the ring. Things from Hunter about how important the little things are, about what really counts in a match. If anything has set me apart, that's what it is. I've tried to put the lessons I learned into practice.

I've worked hard to get where I am, very hard, but I don't forget where I've come from, and I sure don't forget the people who have really given me the lessons and chances I needed to succeed.

I'm not this extremely talented savior of wrestling that some people either think I am or, much worse, think that *I* think I am. I'm Batista.

BOOKER AND ME

But as I was saying, King Booker and I had a little trouble generating some heat when I first came back. Besides our personal difficulties, I think that one of the things that made it hard for us had to do with the way our two characters worked off each other—or didn't. I've always been the kind of babyface who can be easily disliked. Remember, the fans turned me from a heel, and I still have a lot of heel characteristics. I never really changed anything major about the way I worked. I didn't change much about my wrestling style, except to sell it a little more. And I'm not Mr. Personality. I'm not Mr. Ha-ha.

Booker, on the other hand, is one of those heels who's so entertaining, he just makes you laugh. He's hard to dislike. He really is. Just because he's so entertaining, he makes you laugh. It's hard to hate a heel like that who's entertaining the hell out of you. So I think fans were caught in the middle there a little. They couldn't really feel that strongly about me, because they didn't want to hate Booker. And they couldn't really hate him, because my character wasn't someone they could identify with.

Finding the right balance can be awfully difficult.

CHAMP AGAIN

Booker and I worked up to *SummerSlam 2006*, where we fought for the title. We had a thing where I thanked him for holding on to "my" title, and he of course objected. The showdown was inevitable.

Becoming champion the second time could never be as sweet as the first. But it was still a fantastic honor. It means a lot to be champion, whoever you are, but especially for me.

I still had—have—a lot to learn. That's the great thing about wrestling: there's so much to it that you almost have to grow as you go along.

When I first moved up to WWE, I was pretty much like a robot. I knew how to do all the moves, but I couldn't tell you why I was doing them. I would move from A to B to C, going through the steps but not really understanding what they were about. There was no rhyme or reason, at least in my head, to my moves. I didn't pay attention to the crowd; I didn't understand the story that I was trying to tell them. It made for bad wrestling matches.

You could hear it on the mike, too. I was pretty much memorizing things, using words I wouldn't use. They came across like I was reading a script. Badly.

Then as I went further along, especially with the help of Ric and Hunter, I learned how to figure out the story and kind of feed off the crowd. At that point, it started to become more of an art.

When I became champion the first time, I was still learning about that art, still getting a feel for the crowd. Winning the championship belt back, I was able to use my understanding of the story much better. The story of a guy who loses his title to an injury—that's a story anyone can relate to. If they lose their spot at work or on a baseball team or whatever, they know a little bit of what it feels like. Part of my art as a wrestler was to use my story to connect with their story. That's what made people cheer for me, why they wanted me to win, why I was the babyface.

You're creating a piece of art while you're in the ring. I don't know that I've created a masterpiece yet, but I'm definitely working on it.

That's the cool thing about this business. You create something new every day, and you learn by it. Even Vince McMahon says he still learns to this day.

YOUR TIME IS MY TIME

One of the things I've learned only recently is that you don't really want to rush your crowd. Especially if you're in a heated angle with somebody. You want to let things simmer and build gradually. It has to do with the story you're telling. It has to have a satisfying shape.

Some wrestlers are excited when they see that the crowd is already standing on their feet as soon as they get in the ring. For me, I'd rather build a match and bring them to their feet at the end. You know, once you start with them already up, where do you go from there? How do you build that?

That's another thing I learned, actually. The way you build that is you slow it back down and start all over. And again, it has to do with listening to the crowd, letting them tell you where you should go.

But I guess the thing that I keep learning, over and over again, is something that Hunter told me: *everything doesn't have to be an elaborate spot.* It doesn't have to be a car wreck. The more realistic you make it, the better the chance you have of sucking the crowd in.

Being realistic means a lot of times being "small." Wrestlers will punch each other twenty times in the face instead of drawing back and giving that one big punch that takes the guy down realistically. When he falls and sells it, that's a real score with the crowd. In real life, you punch somebody in the face—you know, get a good solid shot on them—they're probably going to drop to the ground. So in a match, that simple shot can have more impact than twenty hard smashes to the face.

SUMO

As a big guy, I've always liked sumo. I could sit for hours and watch sumo. It's just one of those things. The rituals that they have are very cool. The technical aspects are very interesting.

When we were in Japan, I got to see and meet some sumo wrestlers. I'm a big fan of Akebono, and he came to one of our shows and put on a match with Big Show at *WrestleMania 21*. Just to give you a little taste of how good Akebono is, he was the first non-Japanese wrestler to reach the highest rank in sumo, Yokozuna. He held that rank for roughly eight years, which is an eternity in sumo. At six eight and 517 pounds, he had incredible strength and could dominate a match in minutes if not seconds.

The slap on my thighs that I do as part of my entrance is actually a rip-off of sumo, a kind of a tribute to the art form.

While I'm thinking about it, the machine-gun thing I do with my hands, as if I'm firing a pair of H&K MP5Ns as the pyro goes off, came from a suggestion from Shane McMahon.

I'm still kind of uncomfortable speaking in front of people. I don't know if I went out and was kind of the goofball I am, I don't know how people would take that—my character is kind of serious. But I get through it.

When my mother originally told some of our family friends that I was going to be a pro wrestler, they were all pretty surprised.

"But he doesn't talk!" they all said. "He'll be great and everything, but doesn't he actually have to speak?"

I guess I have a reputation for being pretty quiet in the family, especially compared to everyone else. As a matter of fact, a lot of our friends and even my mom were surprised when they first started seeing me on the show, because compared to at home, I talk a ton on TV.

They used to write all this stuff for me. They'd give me five paragraphs and I'd condense it into two sentences. So they pretty much gave up on writing things for me and just gave me bullet points to make. I just go out and make my point. I try to speak from the heart. I think people can connect with that. They know I'm just saying what I feel. I'm never going to be like The Rock. Like Hogan. I'm never going to be Mr. Excitement. That's just not me. I'm more mild-mannered, more soft-spoken. I just kind of try and be myself, make my point, and get the hell out of there.

WORKING OUT

My look has always been my strong point. I'm the first to tell people that it was how I got my job. I don't try to fool people and say I worked really hard as a wrestler and paid my dues on the indies. I got my job because I was built like a brick shit house. They took a look at me and said, Well, let's give it a try.

So it's pretty critical that I keep that look, even as I get older. Luckily for me, staying in shape has been an easy part of my wrestling career. I've really centered my life around working out. I don't even think about it. It's something that's in my everyday daily routine.

And I love working out. I do it every day in some way, shape, or form. It hasn't been a chore for me.

It can be hard while you're on the road. You have to make the time, you have to somehow forget how tired you are, and you have to find the gym.

That's one thing I've always loved about Kane. He's an encyclopedia of gyms. If you're ever in a town and you need to know where the gym is, you just ask Kane. Not only does he know where it is, he's probably been there already. He can give you a rundown of all the machines and programs they've got, what's nearby, whatever you need.

I've learned to become very antisocial when I go to the gym. It's not because I'm a prick or anything. It's because if one person comes up and starts talking to me, that opens the door for everybody else to come up to start talking to me. Ordinarily I wouldn't mind, except that when I'm on the road, I'm usually very time restricted. I may have only forty-five minutes or less to work out. I have to do my thing and go. I really don't have time to socialize at the gym; I'm basically there to do my job. So a lot of times, I'll be very standoffish. I slap on my headphones and try purposely not to make eye contact with anybody. It's just something I've learned that I've had to do to be able to go places and get through my workout without being in there for three hours.

I know some people take it the wrong way and think I'm a dick. But it's something I've had to learn to do.

TAG TEAMS

A lot of the big matches I've had in my career, and certainly while I've been champion, were singles matches, but I still love working in tag teams. Working tags always seems to be more fun. I don't know why.

They are definitely easier physically, because you are able to tag in and out. You can catch your breath and rest out of the spotlight a little bit. But they're harder in a lot of other ways. There's a lot going on, especially if they're six-man tags or even eight-man tags, which we did a lot of when I was in Evolution. Then you have so many people going in there that it can easily get confusing. You have to focus on creating your story, making your part of the match come alive.

I've had some great tag team partners over the years. I talked earlier about Ric Flair and how flattered I am to have my name linked with his in wrestling history. I like the things that connect me to other people, to other great wrestlers.

One of the great wrestlers I tagged with was Rey Mysterio. Working with Rey was so much fun. Sometimes I would get lost in the corner just watching him, just being amazed at the things he was able to do. He's so incredibly talented. He's an amazing athlete. He really is. I turned into a fan sitting there in the corner.

Rey's a legend in the cruiserweight division, and helped make the cruiserweight contests one of the most popular segments of the WCW programming during the Monday Night Wars back when both WCW and our company were competing in the late nineties. He came over to us in 2002. His athletic ability is phenomenal. He's had so many great matches, but I think a lot of fans will remember his work with Eddie Guerrero for years and years.

His career has been amazing. But as a person, as a husband, as a father, that's where his greatness lies. If you saw him with his kids, you'd know he's just an incredible man.

Rey and I worked with MNM for a long time. MNM was a tag team of Joey Mercury and Johnny Nitro, with Melina as their manager.

We had so much fun with those guys. For one, Nitro and Mercury are very talented. But Melina really made it fun.

Her character is such a raging bitch. The arena just loved to see her embarrassed or humiliated. We'd always end the matches with her hanging over the ropes and her ass hanging out there. She'd always wear these little skirts and tiny thongs, her little butt hanging out.

We'd do a spot where Rey would set the three of them up for a 6-1-9, one of his signature moves. The 6-1-9 is Rey's version of a Tiger feint, where he jumps through the ropes and uses the momentum to swing back into the ring. You see it in Japan and Mexico a lot. You have to be pretty athletic to do it, but of course Rey's got the juice to pull it off. The name, 6-1-9, is a reference to the area code of San Diego, where Rey was born.

He would hit Melina last. She'd end up hanging over the ropes, and we'd leave her there for a little while so we and the rest of the arena could get a good eyeful of her ass. Then usually we'd end the match with me rolling Nitro and Mercury out of the ring, leaving Melina there. I'd ask her for a little kiss.

She'd give me a slap. Then she'd turn around and Rey would grab her, spin her, and dip her. Of course, she's taller than he is, so that was always good for a laugh. He'd bend her over for the big dip and give her the big kiss and she'd fall on her ass and oversell it.

A WARM-UP

The night Rey and I won the Tag Team Championship from MNM, there was supposed to be a locker-room scene where Melina came in and tried to seduce me before the match, hoping to get me to call the match off. The way it was originally written, I was supposed to say, "Fuck you. Go away," and turn her down.

Our head writer, Michael Hayes, came up to me before the show and said, "Let me ask you a question. If a hot girl came into your locker room and offered you some, would you really turn her down?"

"Well, I don't know," I said, thinking about it. "Probably not."

"Would your character turn it down?"

"*Hell no!*"

"Well, you might want to mention that."

So I went to Stephanie McMahon, who's in charge of creative for the company.

"Look, it's kind of cheesy," I told her. "What kind of puss would I be if a hot girl came into my locker room and offered me some and I sent her away? That's not cool. I think the guys in the audience want to see me, you know, hit it."

So she went and talked to Vince, and they changed the whole thing for me. Instead of turning Melina down, I got some in the locker room.

Of course, then Melina came out and said, "We have a deal, right?"

"No, we don't have a deal," I told her, "but that was a hell of a warm-up. Thanks, I'm going to go and kill those guys."

Which I did.

STORY LINES

Sometimes we don't know what the hell we're doing until we show up the day of the show, because things are constantly changing. Ideas pop into somebody's head. Guys get injured. It's like a constant machine that's always going.

It all starts from a concept. The thing with me turning on Hunter, for example: it all sparked when we teased that turn. Then the writers went to work. They came up with things to take that concept forward. The story line built as we went.

Usually I'll get a call from the agents, or the head writer, Sunday or Monday. They'll let me know what's going on. We shoot *SmackDown!* on Tuesdays, taping it so it can be aired on Friday. By the time I get to the arena Tuesday, I have a good idea what's on the table.

Michael Hayes is our head writer. He's done wonders since he took over as head writer of *SmackDown!*

Hayes wrestled as Michael P.S. Hayes—P.S. stood for "Purely Sexy." His career in the ring ran from the seventies to the nineties. He was with the National Wrestling Alliance—NWA—where at one point he was teamed up with Ric Flair. He also wrestled with WCW before joining our company in the late nineties as a manager and then a commentator. He's been head writer at *SmackDown!* since October 2006.

I'll talk to him, say what I like and what I don't like about the script, and he'll go back to Vince, who always has the final say-so on what goes on. So it's one big collaboration, with Vince having the final word.

MELINA

Melina and I have become pretty good friends, close physically since my divorce as well as emotionally. But when she and I first started working together, I didn't like her very much. I don't think she liked me very much either.

I think a lot of people don't realize that by nature I'm a quiet guy. They think that if I don't start chitchatting with them, I somehow don't like them. There's some situations where I'm really just shy, especially with women. That's just not in some people's nature—some guys could have a conversation with a lamppost and make it interesting. So they don't really understand where I'm coming from.

On the other hand, I also have a bit of an attitude toward people new to the business. I think they should be very humble, very respectful to the people who have been in the company awhile.

What I think happened between Melina and me was, because of our separate perspectives, there was a misunderstanding. She's very friendly and thinks that anyone who doesn't talk to her somehow doesn't like her. And one day after she'd started working with MNM, she came up to me and started crying. She said she didn't know why I didn't like her. It absolutely broke my heart. The differences in our personalities had gotten in the way.

I think that's something that happens not just in wrestling. A lot of times people don't take the time or make the effort to understand where someone else is coming from. The truth is, I hadn't taken the time to know who Melina was. She comes across as this evil diva vixen on television. That's her character. But in real life, she's really just very sweet. She's very mild-mannered.

Women in wrestling have a hard time being accepted, but many have really worked hard to get where they are. Yes, there are girls who get into wrestling because of contests and are chosen primarily because of their looks. But from what I've seen, the ones who really advance and stick around, the real divas, put an incredible amount of work into what they do.

In Melina's case, she trained with an old-timer named Jesse Hernandez and learned how to work before she joined the company. She really knows the psychology of the business. You can sit down with her and talk for hours about storytelling, and she just gets it.

My wife thought I was sleeping with Melina right off the bat, while we were still married. It wasn't true, but it did make me feel guilty about being friends with her.

Since then, as I've said, Melina and I have gotten closer and our relationship has become physical. That's caused a bit of controversy, but I don't give a shit. She's my friend, and I love her very much.

OMAHA

The crowd at Omaha's Qwest Arena is really up for the show, and Kennedy and I give them a good match, Ken riling them up until I finally slam the door on him.

It was a great match.

How great?

Stone Cold called up Kennedy later and said, "I loved the shit out of that match."

You can't get any higher praise than that.

Meanwhile, Undertaker gets a big pop from the crowd in his segment on the same show. I can tell that's a sign of things to come. He and I are going to be working our butts off over the next few months, heading toward our showdown at *WrestleMania*. I'm the champ; he's undefeated at *'Mania*. Something's got to give.

Ten

ROAD STORIES

Life as a wrestler involves a huge amount of time on the road. Partly because of that, and partly because of the image wrestlers have gotten in the media, people think that it's all one big party.

It's not. Most times not only am I exhausted after a show, but I have to drive a couple of hours to get to the next city before I go to sleep.

But there are exceptions. And those exceptions make great stories, which of course everyone likes to hear.

I'll take a shot at telling a few without sending too many people to jail.

RECOGNITION FACTOR

A lot of my really good stories involve Ric Flair, who had a reputation as a serious partier long before I joined the business. He just seems to attract a good time.

And women. All the women love Ric.

First of all, I want to say we didn't frequent strip clubs a lot. But one time, Ric and I found ourselves in one in South Carolina. I forget exactly what the circumstances were, but the owner met us at the door and took us inside, then showed us back to the VIP section.

There wasn't any funny business; it was a legal place. But those girls were completely without clothes. And before you knew it, every stripper in the club had left the stage, the poles, their lap dances, and whatever they were doing. They all came back to be with us in that room. We had a blanket of naked women hanging all over me and Ric.

Which I'm sure made the fifty or sixty guys in the rest of the club pretty pissed.

RIC'S PARTY

I know there are all these stories out there about Ric doing outrageous things. I don't want to say that he's a changed man since he got married, but maybe being in love with the right woman has altered his behavior a little. His wife, Tiffany, is really something.

Ric got married while I was out injured. I wanted to do something nice for him, give Ric a bachelor party, so I started planning one while we were having a supershow in D.C., which is my hometown. I figured all the boys would be there, and we'd give him a good send-off for his marriage.

Tiffany said no way. She told me he'd had a bachelor party for the last thirty years, and his bachelor party days were over.

So we changed it to an engagement party.

It was a hell of a good time. I rented a club run by guys I used to work for, and they were gracious enough to give me a very good deal. We had every kind of food you can imagine, and a really hot DJ. We were pouring huge bottles of Cristal all night. Every time a new bottle came out, there would be fireworks on the tray so you could see it across the dance floor.

At every party Ric has ever been to, he clears a circle in the middle of the dance floor and makes room for himself to dance. And more times than not, he ends up in that circle with less clothes on than when he started.

Sometimes a *lot* less.

Tiffany hopped right up when he reached for his belt at the party. You could see people getting knocked over as she came through the crowd. She grabbed his hand and shook her finger at him, as if he were a bad dog.

"No. No. No," she said. And that was that. Ric's clothes stayed on that night.

She wasn't mad or anything. She loves Ric for who he is. But now that he's married, he's living by higher standards.

RANDY

Another guy that just seems to be a magnet for women is Randy Orton.

I remember one time we were in Albany, Georgia, and I had just left the show. I was looking for something to eat, so I stopped at a Lone Star Steakhouse or a Texas Roadhouse or something along those lines. I went in and saw that Maven and Randy were already there. So I walked over and what did I see but this really smoking hot blonde sitting in Randy's lap.

I said hello and introduced myself to her. There was a guy standing by the booth and I asked who he was.

"I'm with her," he told me.

I asked him if that was his sister. And he said, "No, that's my girl-friend."

I started yelling at him. I told him to get his girlfriend and leave, or he was never going to see her again. Randy would steal her from him.

It was kind of a big joke, and everybody started laughing. Until the girl began kissing Randy.

The boyfriend got a little upset and walked over toward the bar. I felt so bad for the guy, I went and snatched her out of Randy's lap.

It was all in fun, but the more I thought about it, the more I thought that girl was pretty cute. So after we sent her back to the boyfriend, I sent my waitress over to get her phone number.

I ended up seeing her myself a few times. She was sweet.

PORTUGAL

There are a number of women who throw themselves at wrestlers. It's one of those things. Wrestlers get more attention than other athletes. Football players and basketball players don't have the recognition factor we do. Our show airs worldwide, and it's every week, so usually when we go places, people immediately know who we are.

Someone was joking around not too long ago, asking me where the best strip clubs were. I'm not much of an expert, so I don't really know. But from my experience, I can tell you what country has the *worst*.

Portugal. By far.

We were on tour one time there and ended up in a strip club, because there was no place else open. Honest to God. We hopped into a cab one night and asked the taxicab driver to take us to a nightclub. And he took us to a strip club, telling us that was the only place open.

But the deal there, which we didn't know when we went in, was that the strip clubs weren't just strip clubs but whorehouses. At least the one where we were was.

The women may have been hookers, but they had to be the ugliest women I had ever seen. I don't think there was one there without a mustache.

We didn't stay long. It was one of those times when it was pretty easy to decide you'd be better off back at the hotel, renting a movie.

TOKYO

I'd say by far the country I've had the most fun in while on tour is Japan. Tokyo, specifically. God, I've had so many good times there.

There's a little section right outside the city called Roppongi where there are just blocks and blocks of nothing but bars. They don't close until everyone's done partying. And the Japanese tend to go all night.

One of the women in the company was on tour with us there one time . . .

Maybe I better withhold the names here to protect the guilty . . .

She's just a sweetheart and I love her to death, but she would always try a little too hard to prove that she fit in with the guys. She did this by trying to go drink for drink.

Me and Shane O'Mac at the Hard Rock Café in Tokyo.

Not a good thing when you weigh maybe a hundred pounds. It would take less than an hour for her to pass out at the bar. And she passed out every night.

One night we sat her on a bar stool and kind of carried on without her, dancing, that sort of thing. A whole bunch of us were there. Finally, it came time to go home. We got one of the younger wrestlers to act as her bodyguard, take her back to her hotel and make sure nothing happened to her. As we were sticking her in the cab, it occurred to us that we couldn't let her off *that* easily. I can't tell you half of what we might have done to a guy in that situation.

Somebody said, "Let's shave her eyebrows off."

I had to step up and draw the line.

Her "bodyguard" got her back to the hotel okay and left her to sleep it off. I don't even want to guess what her head felt like the next day. I know she couldn't remember what the hell happened or how she had gotten back to her room or anything from the night.

STILL STANDING

I've always admired the guys who could hang at the all-nighters and still put on a show without looking the worse for it. Ric and Hunter were all-stars. Another person who was great at it was The Hurricane, Gregory Helms. He was always closing down the place. And Chris Jericho. I think he closed down every bar he and I ever went to. He's a true-blue rock star: parties and still gives a five-star match, night after night.

Don't get me wrong. Chris is human like the rest of us. You'd watch him kind of deteriorate a little bit through the week while we were on tour in Europe. He'd start out looking all neat and clean at the beginning of the week; by the end of the week he'd climb on the bus with his hair greasy and his shirt hanging out, missing a couple of buttons. In fact, I've been on tours with him where at the end of the week he stops buttoning his shirt altogether.

But when we'd get to the show, his performance was always right on. He ran on adrenaline. Once it hit, he gave the crowd their money's worth. That's amazing.

Another time we were up in Calgary, Canada. I forget exactly the arrangements but we had done a show somewhere and it was a late night. About two in the morning I was checking into a hotel, along with two guys who were rookies at the time. I think it was the Heart Throbs—Antonio Thomas and Romeo Roselli—who were with us in 2005 and had wrestled earlier in OVW as the Heartbreakers. Anyway, I'm walking up to the desk and I get this call on my cell phone. It was Chris. He asked what I was doing.

"I'm checking into the hotel," I told him.

"No you're not. I'm at this bar down the street. Get your ass down here."

I looked over the rooks and said, "What are you guys doing?"

"We're exhausted," they told me. "We're going to go get some sleep."

"No you're not. You're coming down to the bar with me. If I have to be there you have to be there."

I dragged those poor kids down to the bar. It was kind of an initiation thing. Chris and I thought it would be pretty funny if we fed them some shots to break them in a little bit. They got over with me pretty quick: they not only drank every drink we handed them but still came to work the next day and smiled, never complained or anything.

TWENTY-TWO KAMIKAZES

I guess if I'm really going to give myself up, I ought to confess about the time Shane McMahon and Jonathan Sully were in Thailand doing a promotional tour. Shane, of course, has been on both sides of the ring, and has a pretty important executive position with the company as executive vice president of Global Media. Jonathan works in our British office.

We'd had a long day of seeing people and had had a long day. We decided to go out after dinner and have a few drinks.

We went to what looked like a respectable bar in a hotel. It was packed when we went in. Shane and I concentrated on our drinks. For some reason we started drinking kamikazes. We polished off twenty-two each in an hour, which for me was a record.

Shane's a competitive guy.

The next day, I had to go out and work. This being Thailand, it was smoldering hot. God, it must've been a hundred and ten degrees. And humid. I was hungover and I was sweating and I swear I must have had a mild case of alcohol poisoning.

HELSINKI

One time Hunter, Chris Jericho, Ric Flair, and I were sitting in a bar in Helsinki, Finland. We were smoking big cigars and we noticed people passing by giving us shitty looks. We couldn't figure out why. We thought maybe because we looked and sounded like Americans, and the people didn't like Americans.

Then we realized there was this huge sign right over our heads that said "No Smoking."

I'd like to say it was in Finnish, but it was in English. We just hadn't noticed it.

Since we'd already started, we figured what the hell and went on smoking.

The next night—really the next morning, since it would have been about three o'clock—I'd gone up to bed so I could grab a short nap before getting up for the airport. I hadn't even hit the pillow when I got a call from one of our referees.

"I have these two girls here who want to meet you."

I thought he was joking with me so I gave him hell and hung up. He called me right back.

"No, I'm serious. These two girls have been looking all over town for you."

I didn't really trust him but I asked what they looked like.

"Well, they're smoking hot. They're beautiful."

So I said go ahead, bring them up.

It turned out he wasn't lying. They were both absolutely drop-dead gorgeous. And they both apparently were fans and had been looking around to find me.

One of them was pretty hammered. The other, though, was pretty sober and I decided why not get to know her a little bit.

Alone, of course.

I thought it would be pretty funny to send the other girl down to Edge's room as a joke. So I had someone bring her down to him.

Edge didn't seem to have his usual sense of humor that night. A few minutes later, just as we were getting comfortable, my new friend got a call on her cell phone.

"The Edge threw me out," said the drunken girl. "The Edge no like me."

Turned out, the friend had decided to take her clothes off in Edge's room, which really annoyed him, so he tossed her clothes in the hall and told her to get the hell out.

THE INTERNET

More and more of our business these days involves the Internet somehow. But I'm one of those guys who has become very anti-Internet, at least as far as the websites and other things concerning wrestlers go. I had my own website for a while but eventually I just stopped participating. There's too much negativity. There are a lot of people out there who all they want to do is rip you apart. It doesn't matter what you do or say, they're going to find some sort of problem with it. And I take that to heart.

You really can't believe everything you read on the Internet. Some wrestlers make it work for them, but I'm still wary. Things just show up from nowhere.

One time, Chris Jericho thought that my clothesline looked so devastating that he could use it as a knockout, as if he'd really been knocked unconscious. He wanted to use it as a shoot and then see if it would get on the Internet. So I went along with it—it's hard not to go along with one of Chris's suggestions. We did the bit and he sold it as a knockout. I went to pick him up as if I thought it was just a work. He was deadweight, as if he was really unconscious. He even had the ref use one of the signs we use when someone's really hurt to get the medical people over.

Sure enough, the next day it was on the Internet that I had *really* knocked him out.

I will say one thing: it sure got my clothesline over. After that, I used it as a finisher for quite a while.

But overall, I don't like the negativity you read online. That why I stopped reading any type of dirt sheets, the so-called newspapers that cover the industry. I think they're all crap. You're usually being ripped apart by fourteen-year-old kids who think they know everything, or guys who could never make it in the business and so are just putting the hate on everyone. I just don't want to have anything to do with that. Too negative.

SIGN GUY

That doesn't mean that true fans can't dislike you or even hate you. On the contrary. And it's great when they can have some fun doing it.

One of the best fans around, a guy who belongs in the hall of fame of fans, is Sign Guy. He got the name because he always brings signs to the shows, and he's a regular at certain big events. He's really loud and he always sits in the front row. He must spend a lot of money to come to our shows. He's really a great character and we've gone so far as to offer to give him tickets, but he's never accepted. He buys his own tickets and makes his own way. That's part of who he is. He's very passionate about our business.

He is brutal on the heels and cheers for the babyfaces. When I was in Evolution, he would just give me hell.

He's had some great signs. One said, "Message for Batista." It had a big hole in the middle of it. I came down the ramp and into the ring and saw it. I didn't quite understand so I stopped and stared at it, trying to figure out what the hell it was supposed to mean.

As soon as he knew he had my attention, he put his hand through it and gave me the finger.

He had another sign when I was making my big babyface turn. Normally he roots for babyfaces, but in my case he hadn't quite made up his mind.

The sign said "Do I Like Batista?" It had one big box that said "Yes." And another big box that said "No."

When I came out, he looked at me and I looked at him.

I gave him a dirty look, so he took a marker out and v-e-r-y slowly checked the "No" box.

SIGN GUY'S HATS

But my best stories about Sign Guy have to do with his hats.

Sign Guy always wears a red cap. He has like a little uniform going, red baseball cap and an Elvis-style gas station shirt. Anyway, one time we were at Madison Square Garden for a television show. We'd gone off the air but we were still in the arena, doing a few last bits for the fans.

Sign Guy had been on us all night. Hunter and I decided to give him hell. So Hunter went down and snatched his hat off his head. I think at first he threw it on the ground and stepped on it a little bit. Then he rubbed it on his ass.

Then it was my turn. I took it and shoved it down the front of my trunks and ran it down and around up the back. It took a while because my trunks aren't too roomy.

Hunter took it gingerly with two fingers, holding it out like it was radioactive, and placed it back on Sign Guy's head.

I think Sign Guy showed up a week or two later with the hat in a plastic bag. It was pinned to a sign that said something like, "growing mold for a science project."

Sometime after that I was in a match with Shelton Benjamin and we were out on the floor right in front of Sign Guy. Shelton was a babyface and was beating the crap out of me. Shelton reached up and snatched the hat from Sign Guy and shoved it down my trunks. Sign Guy was completely surprised because he didn't think a babyface would do that to him. I'm pretty sure he enjoyed the hell out of it, though. From that point on, he started bringing half a dozen hats to the shows, just in case.

But my best Sign Guy story as far as I'm concerned didn't happen in the ring. One time we were in Houston, Texas, and I'd gone out to eat with

Vito LaGrasso. We went to an IHOP that turned out to be right next to a Hooters. We saw Sign Guy sitting at Hooters having something to eat.

That was too easy a target. I snuck on into Hooters and grabbed one of the waitresses. I paid her a hundred bucks to go and take his hat off his head, rub it on her ass, and say, "Batista says hello."

I understand he wasn't all that thrilled about it.

SHOWDOWN WITH UNDERTAKER

One of the biggest story lines I was involved in during 2007 was with Undertaker, a conflict that took us up to *WrestleMania 23*. He and I began working together a few months, leading up to a confrontation with Cena and Shawn Michaels at *No Way Out*. We had a falling-out beforehand—which contributed to Cena pinning 'Taker at *No Way Out*—and headed into a showdown at *Wrestle-Mania*.

Our key confrontation began at a *Raw* show in February 2007, right around the time I started on this book.

On the *Raw* show, we did a thing where John Cena, Bobby Lashley, and myself went out and Undertaker chose from among us for a *WrestleMania* opponent. He chose his opponent by chokeslamming me to the canvas, which is a heck of a way to say let's rumble. The crowd got into it. I think for one thing, they didn't expect two guys from *SmackDown!*, both of whom were babyfaces, to fight. And they knew that Undertaker was undefeated, and that I was champion, so it was going to be a great match no matter what happened.

But there were a couple of things that I was disappointed with.

I was really hoping that we would make the announcement on *SmackDown!* I'm a *SmackDown!* guy and Undertaker's a *SmackDown!* guy, and I was hoping we could make it there.

We're the same company, but there is some competition between the shows. I think it was a little unfair not just to the wrestlers but to the fans. And it would have been a hell of a show for *SmackDown!*

Our viewers deserve the best show possible. There's definitely an overlap in the audiences, but a lot of the people who tune into *SmackDown!* really only have that one chance a week to watch wrestling, and I felt that they deserved this show. It's not just me being competitive with *Raw*. I think part of my job is to stick up for the fans and give them a voice.

My character was really developed on *Raw* and I still feel a lot of loyalty to the show and the guys there. But at the same time, I'm at *SmackDown!* now and I have to take responsibility and help lead the way there. I take a lot of pride in that.

But it's not my decision to make. After I give my opinion—politely—other people get to decide. That's their job.

QUESTIONS MAKE THE STORY

I also thought the physicality between Undertaker and myself came too soon. It immediately put our *No Way Out* match in a different light and put a damper on the big picture. It also took a little of my credibility away. Going into *WrestleMania*, against Undertaker's 14–0 record there, I felt I needed all the credibility I could get. The fact that it was going to be a babyface-babyface match made it even more important that I be considered a legitimate contender. I wanted people to believe that I could stand up to him.

The great thing about me and Hunter going into *WrestleMania 21* was that there were so many unanswered questions coming into the show. We'd hardly even touched, let alone had a match. So I think that the fans really wanted to know what the answers were going to be. We left them wanting to see that physicality, wanting to get their questions answered. Here we started out with an answer, really—Undertaker snagging me and chokeslamming me tells you he has the upper hand.

I had no problem with the chokeslam itself; it was where it came in the story. It doesn't really matter to me whether people are booing me or cheering—I want them to be entertained. I want them to watch the show. It's about the big picture.

I wasn't too happy about it, but it was one of those things where Vince had a feeling on it, and we have to go with that. We have to trust him, because obviously the man knows what he's doing.

WRESTLEMANIA

The *WrestleMania* match was a dream come true for me. I'd been on the road for weeks promoting it—it was the month from hell—and of course I knew what the outcome was going to be, but when we got to Detroit it was just unbelievable. Over eighty thousand people. It was incredible.

I was so psyched up because working with 'Taker was a dream match of mine. It couldn't've worked out any better. Everything we did was just great.

Even though I was dropping the title, it still felt good. The year before, when I had to surrender it because of injuries, that was just fucking brutal that night. If I have to drop the championship belt, I want to drop it right in the middle of the ring. I think every good wrestler wants to do that. That's the way it should be.

This was our first match ever. Leading up to it we had a house show and a triple threat; during that, we had about five seconds of interaction. But we didn't want to give away too much. Nobody had ever seen us go.

Even though we'd never worked together, we just had automatic chemistry at *WrestleMania*. It was just a magic night.

When I made my entrance, it took forever to get to the ring. The arena and stage were so damn big. I had to stand in the ring and catch my breath for a minute. Then Undertaker started making his entrance—it was so damn eerie. It didn't seem real. I turned to Charles Robinson, who was our ref, and said, "This is like a dream."

A scary one.

The match was fifth, which 'Taker and I both felt was kind of a slap

Leaving
Undertaker to
the mercy of
Cena and HBK.

in the face. I thought our match had really sold. Our story was the biggest story going into 'Mania. Putting us on fifth was a little insulting.

When I found out we were going to be fifth, Michael Hayes and Pat Patterson were there. Pat said, "It might be a good thing. Do you want to follow Shawn?"

Meaning Shawn Michaels, who was wrestling John Cena for the WWE title in what became the final match.

Automatically I said, "Fuck yeah, we want to follow Shawn. We can follow anybody."

Pat Patterson died laughing because he loves the cockiness and competitiveness of wrestlers, but I did truly believe we could follow anybody.

I should say that for a lot of my better matches, the biggest matches of my career, I've had Michael Hayes and Pat Patterson working with me as agents. They were both on my *WrestleMania 23* match with Undertaker, and my Hell in a Cell match with Triple H. I want to thank them for that. They've helped me tremendously.

But I guess management didn't think we were the main event at that *WrestleMania*. I think we proved them wrong, because the fans really responded to us. I thought we stole the show, and that our match was by far the best of the night.

A lot of times big guy–big guy things sound good on paper—you think it's going to be the clash of the titans, but I don't know, they just don't come off. They just don't gel. But even

though 'Taker is taller and heavier than I am, he works like a hundred and fifty pounder, and I think that was one of the keys to this match. He was just amazing. In fact, I learned a lot from him just by working with him. I felt kind of like a sponge, absorbing his lessons.

At one point in the match he hit me with a shoot right hook that got me right on the jaw. "Shoot" as in real, as in son of a bitch, that mother hurt.

He got me right on the fuckin' button. You can tell if you watch it carefully. I fell back against the ropes, kind of dazed. He knocked me silly. I was dizzy, and it took me a couple of seconds to clear my head.

I thought it was just a potatoey slip, no big deal, but when I came back to throw the next big punch he said, "That was a receipt. You broke my eardrum."

I said, "Oh fuck, I'm sorry."

"No, no, come on, man. Come on," he told me, and we carried on from there.

I still don't know where it happened. I didn't ask, either—it's one of those things you don't want to keep bringing up.

When I came off after the match, I screamed out to Pat Patterson and anyone else who could hear, "Fuckin' follow that." I knew we'd had a great show.

Besides the story coming in, we had so many milestones in that match. 'Taker has never held the World Heavyweight title; he's held the WWE title but never the World. We had never worked with each other. It was a big babyface-versus-babyface match. And it was the first time anybody had ever kicked out of my finish.

I don't know where 'Taker is in his career. From what I've heard, he may be winding it down, and if so this was his last big title run. To me, that's got main event written all over it. I thought we should have ended that show with Undertaker holding the championship belt in the air.

But I think we stole the show anyway.

The only way it could get better would be if it were a Hell in a Cell match. That's my next dream match, Hell in a Cell with the Dead Man.

DREAM MATCHES

Speaking of dream matches—one of the guys I would have just loved to have been in the ring with in his prime was Hulk Hogan.

I have no idea what a match with him would have been like. He doesn't have to do a whole lot to get the fans involved. They're automatically sucked in. I would imagine that if we had a match, it would have been him kicking my ass a whole lot. Me bouncing around for him like a Ping-Pong ball. Then somewhere at the end, it would have been me lying on my back.

But it would have been a great match.

There's a lot of guys that I would have loved to be in the ring with. Can you imagine tag teaming Arn Anderson? Hell, I wish I could just crawl inside of Arn's brain for ten minutes. It'd be incredible.

I'm such a big Four Horsemen mark, I would have loved to have been part of that.

Stone Cold is another guy that I would have loved to wrestle with during his prime. Just the electricity he generates is incredible. I told him that recently and his answer was, "Ah, I was just havin' fun."

DON'T LET ME FORGET CHAVO OR DUSTY

I just realized that I've written nearly the entire book and not mentioned either Chavo Guerrero or Dusty Rhodes. They're two great guys who have been incredibly important to me.

Chavo—also known as Chavo Jr.—is the son of wrestler Chavo Guerrero (aka Chavo Sr., aka Chavo Classic), Eddie Guerrero's brother. Wrestling is in that family's genes. If I could choose a brother, I'd choose Chavo Guerrero. Enough said.

Wrestling fans probably most remember Dusty Rhodes for his legendary feuds with the Four Horsemen. Now he works behind the scenes as a booker. Dusty has not only been a very strong influence in my career but I also believe that he is the coolest human being on the face of the Earth. And that's really saying something, because I've met a lot of people.

I'm not lumping them together—they're pretty different guys, each with his own achievements—but I don't want to let this book go without mentioning them and how much they mean to me.

BACKLASH

The sequel to *WrestleMania 23*, *Backlash*, featured another great match between 'Taker and me. We were debating on the finish right up until the end. We were doing a huge stunt at the end—a spear from me that drove us both off the stage, flying down and ending up unconscious. It sounded incredible, but when we went through it in rehearsal we weren't that impressed with it. We were debating right up until the end to decide what the ending would be. We were literally talking about it on our way to the ring. Undertaker said keep your ears open, we might pull an audible at the end. But it came off so good that it would have been completely unnecessary to add on.

We were both injured coming into the match. Most people knew about my hamstring tear.

It had happened a few weeks before, when I was in Europe doing a match with Fit Finlay. It was obvious right away; I tried rubbing it out but I could barely get through the match. It wasn't serious enough to have surgery, but it definitely had an effect on my wrestling; hamstring injuries are hard to work with. They don't heal up very fast.

I wrestled with tape on my leg for a few weeks. The funny thing about that is, some guy on the Internet was convinced—absolutely convinced—that I was faking the injury and wore the tape to cover a new tattoo. He was absolutely positive that I had a new tattoo I didn't know about.

Anyway, Undertaker tore his biceps on the same tour. Kane and MVP were also hurt. As a matter of fact, we had to start doing six-man Tag Team matches on the tour to camouflage the injuries that a lot of us had. At one point, I think only Fit Finlay wasn't hurt.

Wait, I take that back: he had his thumbnail ripped off. He had a big bandage on it—we ribbed him good for that. We're all beat up—me with my leg, 'Taker with his arm, MVP with his back, and Fit with the bad thumbnail . . .

It was a tough tour. We did something like twelve cities in twelve days.

There were detours everywhere, and Italy had this new law where you couldn't have a bathroom on a bus, so we were constantly stopping: a two-hour ride would take six hours at least.

When we got back, Undertaker knew that he was going to have to have surgery after *Backlash*, because his biceps was completely detached at the tendon. So we had one final Cage match on TV, because we couldn't wait for the next Pay-Per-View, which was the original plan. Undertaker had only a small window of opportunity to get his biceps fixed before it couldn't be fixed at all.

It's too bad, because the original plan was great. We were going to have a Cage match that would end up in a draw again. Then the Pay-Per-View after that we were going to do the Hell in a Cell showdown that I've always dreamed of. But we had to get the title off 'Taker because he was going into surgery and was going to be out for a while.

I worked with 'Taker a lot in 2007, before his surgery. Everywhere we went, we tore the house down. It was such a good learning experience for me. 'Taker is truly a ring general. He's also a real good guy. We had a chance to hang out, have a few drinks together on tour. I mentioned earlier that I had some heat with him when I came over to *SmackDown!* because of some things I said. I think he's finally forgiven me for that, and I think he enjoyed working with me.

Every night after a match he'd say he was proud of me. It may seem like a simple thing, but for me being in there and earning his respect—it's icing on the cake. I put everything, my passion, my soul, into this business, and having someone with the legendary status of Undertaker saying he's proud of you, having his approval: I can't put it into words, I guess.

I know he was crushed about giving up the title. No one wants to give up the title because of an injury, especially someone like Undertaker, who's so proud. And at the same time, we had such a good thing going that it was a real heartbreaker to have to stop it. Our feud was awesome for *SmackDown!*, awesome for the business.

The first replacement plan called for Kennedy to cash in his Money in the Bank contract, which he had won at *WrestleMania*. He'd have then taken the title. In the meantime, I would have worked into a thing with Fit Finlay before getting my chance to go after the title.

But then we thought that Kennedy had a torn triceps—it turned out

he didn't need surgery, though he was out for several weeks—so we had to change things again. Edge won the Money in the Bank contract from Kennedy, then cashed it in and took the title off of 'Taker in a match that Mark Henry was also involved in.

EDGE

When Edge came in and won the championship, he really was picking bones that night—Undertaker had been wiped out not just by me, but by Mark Henry, who'd come out afterward and made a statement. So the crowd really considered him a heel. He just had tons of heat.

Edge and I worked a lot together when I was in Evolution. He was a big babyface back then and we bounced around a lot for him. In 2007, the story came full circle, with him as heel as I chased the title, trying to get it back.

We hadn't worked in a while, but the chemistry was still there. Actually, I've never seen Edge have bad chemistry with anyone. He's just a great worker. I love working with him. Once you know you're clicking with a guy, it's easy. With the story line we built—him coming in and stealing the title that I was chasing—the crowd was already there. Undertaker and I had had three wars, and they were really mad that he came in and stole that away.

One thing I've always liked about Edge, he takes the crowd on a ride. He'll go back and forth, back and forth, taking them up and down. That can make a real difference—it separates the men from the boys.

MOVIES

Since I got into this business when I was already older than most guys, I understand that my career isn't going to stretch forever into the future. As long as I can stay in shape, I intend on wrestling. But I don't want to get to the point where I'm just doing it to make a paycheck. I want to be able to walk away from this healthy and happy, with all my wits about me. I don't intend on waiting until I've had one too many chair shots to the head.

There are other things I'm interested in. For one, I'm pursuing other aspects of entertainment. I'd really like to branch out and do some movies. I'm really big into superheroes and sci-fi. I can't tell you how jealous I was of Triple H when he got the role of Jarko Grimwood in *Blade: Trinity*, the 2004 movie that pits Blade—a vampire hunter—against a group of vampires out to take over the earth. It's the third movie in the series.

I did get a chance to appear on a television show, *Smallville*, the series that deals with Superman's teenage years, before he heads to Metropolis. It wasn't a very good experience overall, but I did like it because I'm a big superhero buff. And seeing all the details that went on with a production like that was pretty interesting.

I was real intimidated, because I'm not a professional actor. I do a little acting here and there on the show, but I was worried about how the other actors would be toward me. But Tom Welling, who stars as Clark Kent, was more than gracious. He was helpful and very polite, making me feel at ease and giving me a lot of tips.

The part itself was pretty one-dimensional—I was a bone-sucking monster. But in the script, at least, I had a few decent lines that made the character a little bit more interesting.

Of course, most of that got cut out. They even dubbed in a line that I never said, in a totally different voice.

We spent a whole day setting up an elaborate stunt where I threw Superman into a big cargo net and there was a real cool explosion. It made me look a little cool, because I was pretty much kicking Superman's ass. But when it aired, all you could see was me throwing Superman up—then he flew over the crane and he came back down. All the cool effects of the shot were completely lost, and I looked like a little wuss.

I was hoping for a little more.

Another dream of mine is to own a nightclub. I've got a couple of friends who own nightclubs, and they've offered to go into business with me. One of them is David Kareem, who's been a friend of mine since my bouncing days. Back then he was finishing up his education at the University of Maryland. He's gone on now in the business and owns his

He was lucky to get
out in one piece.

own clubs. Every time we see each other, we can't believe how far we've both come.

I wear a sentimental bracelet on my wrist all the time—people ask me about it a lot. It actually belonged to Dave. I always told him how much I liked it. One night he took it off and gave it to me.

"Here," he said. "My father made that for me right before he died."

It was a real sentimental gift. In return, I gave him my wedding ring, which I used to wear around my neck after my divorce. It cost me $26,000 and is completely covered in diamonds, but every time I looked at it, it kind of broke my heart. So I think I got the better end of that deal.

In some ways, it's tempting to go and open a club right now. But so much of my time is focused on wrestling, I just wouldn't be able to. I want to be hands-on. So I think I'll wait until I leave the ring before taking them up on the offer.

I'll definitely be hands-on. You never know, I might throw on the security shirt and stand at the door for a while. Bounce at my own night-club. That'd be great.

FIRST LOVE

Wrestling, though, will always be my first love.

Triple H said something to me one time that made so much sense I've repeated it over and over. He said he wanted to branch out and do other forms of entertainment because it would help bring viewers into wrestling. I thought that just made so much sense. Wrestling really is where my heart is. It's my passion. There's nothing like the thrill of the live crowd. Coming out and performing in front of a wrestling crowd is just incredible. It's a challenge every night to make the crowd stand up on their feet and scream and yell. I can't tell you how thrilled it makes me to meet that challenge.

I hope I'll always have a job in this business in one way, shape, or form. That's what I hope for. When I hang up my boots and leave the ring, I hope that the company will keep me on in some aspect behind the scenes or working with younger talent. I love this company, and I'd love to always have a job here.

But otherwise, most of what I dream about the future holding are good things for my family. I want to be able to give my mom a good life, which she deserves. I don't want her to worry about bills. She struggled so hard for us when we were young. She did her best to keep me alive and out of jail and off the streets. I want to return some of that. I'll never be able to do enough for my mom.

Or my daughters. I have high hopes for Athena. I think she's going to go far in life. And for my older daughter, Keilani, I want her to find happiness. I don't know what she's searching for or what she wants to do with her life, but I hope she finds it.

ROLE MODEL

One of the great things about being a celebrity is that you get a chance to help people in unexpected ways. Nobody told me about it when I started wrestling and it certainly wasn't why I became a wrestler, but it's just very cool.

If you recall, I said I spent some time in a group home when I was a kid. It happens that that group home is still around. A judge there invited me to come up and talk to some of the kids there recently. I did and it was just an awesome experience.

I was quick to point out that I haven't been an angel in my life. I'm not a perfect citizen. If I can be a role model, it's by helping people learn from my mistakes. This way, maybe they can bypass the errors I made. Learn from them. Avoid my problems. Because they may not be as lucky as I've been in the end.

Teenagers have to understand that there is a big world out there, with tons of opportunities. You can't just live in your own small world and ignore everything else. You can't ditch school or get into fights or whatever, just because it feels good at that moment. You have to have your eye on the rest of the world, and your future.

I tell kids to get out there and find that one positive thing in their lives that will make them happy. Start small, with one pursuit. Let it build.

For me, it was weight lifting. It was a way to feel better about myself.

It took out some of my aggression. It was therapy, really. And it helped turn my life around.

A lot of kids will find that in sports, through athletics. Some will find that in books. Some will get what they need by educating themselves. Others may have a passion for entertaining people, acting or singing or dancing. Whatever it is, you want to find that one positive thing that you love and pursue it. That will keep you out of trouble.

HEROES

I still feel like the same guy I was ten years ago. A lot of times I feel insecure, or like a goof. I grew up really tall and kind of gangly; I always felt goofy and awkward. That's why bodybuilding made me feel more confident.

But people now see me as a hero. That has everything to do with wrestling.

Part of it, I think, is the sports connection. We all look up to sports figures, guys who can do incredible things with their bodies. I understand that—baseball great Lou Gehrig, "the Iron Horse," who starred for the Yankees in the 1920s and 1930s as a first baseman and played so many games in a row, shrugging off minor injuries, is my personal hero.

But there's more to it than just the fact that wrestlers have to do wild things with their bodies. At its most basic, pro wrestling is all about good and evil. It's really simple to see. Turn on a show and watch it with no volume. You'll understand what's going on because it's so obvious from the way we tell the story in the ring.

People today need heroes. It doesn't matter where they are in the world. They want to identify with good. And that's why wrestling continues to be so popular, and so powerful a form of entertainment.

I went to the Philippines not too long ago. I'd heard from some Filipino people that I was very popular there. I am half Filipino and I'm proud of my heritage; I have a Filipino flag tattooed on my left shoulder. But I had absolutely no idea how popular I was there because of my background. When I got there, I was mobbed. Everywhere I went, thousands

A star.

and thousands of people showed up for my appearances. It was unlike anything else I had experienced in the world. They stuck me on the roof of this car and paraded me around the streets of Manila. People by the thousands showed up, cheering and waving, just because I have Filipino blood. It was a proud moment for me.

And for them. Because I represent hope, good triumphing over evil, a guy overcoming bad stuff in his past to do the right thing and be successful at it.

That's what people want. That's what heroes are about—showing us the way we can overcome all the bad things that happen to us.

A PRIVILEGE

It's awesome and flattering to be someone who gives other people hope. That's truly a special privilege.

Some of my most touching moments have come while I was working with the USO. I went down to Walter Reed Army Medical Center in Maryland and the Bethesda Naval Hospital in Maryland to visit with soldiers and sailors who'd been wounded. It was humbling to walk in there. These guys have shrapnel in them, or they're missing a limb, but they were all smiles when I walked in.

Now, to me they're the real heroes. They put their lives on the line for us, protecting our freedom. There's no way to repay them. But they were so happy to see me and tell me what big fans they were. It was just awesome.

BEYOND WORDS

There are times when being a wrestler touches you so deeply you can't put it into words.

There was this one kid in Tampa. His name was Alex. He was seven years old. Fit Finlay called me and told me that this little boy had terminal cancer and the doctors had really given up hope. He didn't have all that long to live.

All the kid wanted out of the rest of his life was to meet me.

The funny thing is, he lived about a mile down the road. So I went over to see him.

I was dreading it the whole day. I was thinking, *I'm going to go over there, and this kid's going to have tubes in him, and he's dying, and it's going to break my heart.*

But they had him outside the house. His whole family was there, and they were playing and having a good time. He knew he was sick, but he was happy. He wasn't down and depressed.

A few weeks later, I took my truck over. He wasn't in as good shape, but he was still happy to see me, and he was real impressed with the truck. We had a good time talking, and I really enjoyed being with him.

I told him that the next time I came, I was bringing my motorcycle and we'd have a ride.

I guess if I was a real superhero, I'd've found some way to cure his cancer. The best I could do was make him smile.

And he did.

I was looking forward to coming back with the motorcycle. Unfortunately, Alex died a few days later.

I still remember his smile. For a guy who was once pretty much nothing but a street thug, a guy who's made his living by beating up people and being beaten up himself, it was something like a gift from God.

Roscommon County Library Service
WITHDRAWN
FROM STOCK

OMAHA

SmackDown! over, I head out into the parking garage at the back of the stage area. A couple of production guys look like they need a lift to the hotel, so I have them hop in with me. We thread our way through the traffic and get over to the Doubletree hotel, where most of the WWE contingent is staying. Some of the production people end up down at the bar, but I go straight up to my room. I order a room service meal, have something to eat, and then work for a bit on this book.

Remembering all of these things has really put my life in perspective, even made me a little philosophical, I guess. Here's a poor kid who had to eat burnt bean soup all week, a guy who up until eight years ago didn't have two nickels to rub together. Now he's doing things like getting a police escort in Bangkok, motorcycle cops kicking cars out of the way, sirens blaring . . . or going to the Pentagon as the honored guest of the Joint Chiefs of Staff, eating with all these four- and five-star generals—it's just unbelievable.

I've traveled the world and entertained millions of people. In Europe, where I'll be flying to in a few weeks, I'll be working the crowds like I'm a conductor. They're really big on participation. You point at one side of the audience and they roar, then the other and they roar louder. Sometimes I'll stand in the corner of the ring and realize the crowd is singing. I just watch them. It's like I'm in a dream. And I wonder how I got to be there.

The past four years have been just amazing. The places I've been and the experiences I've had, with bigwigs, dignitaries—it's just amazing for a guy who didn't even finish high school.

People look at the financial success, but that's probably the smallest part of it. It does let me do one thing I really, really love: I always wanted to spoil people. Now I can.

So how did I get here?

There were tons of components, but it started with people believing in me: Angie, Richard Salas, Jonathan Meisner. The list goes on and on. Afa, Jim Cornette, Fit Finlay, Ric, Hunter, and Vince.

And I believed in myself. There were times when I was down, a lot of times, but I dug in. Some of it was out of fear that if I didn't make it, I didn't know what else I would do. But it was more than that. A lot of people were depending on me. I had to do it.

In my heart, I'll always be that poor kid from D.C. At least I hope I will. Because I don't think there's anything wrong with that—I wouldn't want to be anyone else.

But tonight, I'm so tired that my eyes are just about hanging out of my head. This has been a typical, exhausting week. All I really want to do is get on the plane tomorrow and go home. My mom will be there, and most likely she'll have spent the day cooking. She makes these great oatmeal raisin cookies, cakes, you name it. Her meatloaf is great, too.

Finally, I'm done for the night. I close down the laptop. My eyes have shut before I hit the pillow.

COUNTY LIBRARY SERVICE

ROSCOMMON